$3.95
Y A

(continued from front of jacket)

... *conventional. A Britisher and a confirmed civilian, he volunteered, manned a search-light, was commissioned into a proud and ancient regiment, and was transferred into intelligence, where he organized the famous Affair of Monty's Double. He never got out of England.*

Moonlight on a Lake in Bond Street

STEPHEN WATTS

As the *London Sunday Times* says: "Such a career did not bring Mr. Watts into contact with the more spectacular aspects of war, though to be bombed in the Café de Paris is probably as painful an experience as anyone can suffer under fire, and it provides Mr. Watts with the material for one of the most perceptive and best-written chapters in this very well-written book. . . .

[Continued on back flap]

MOONLIGHT ON A LAKE
IN BOND STREET

MOONLIGHT ON A LAKE
IN BOND STREET

STEPHEN WATTS

NEW  YORK

W · W · NORTON & COMPANY · INC ·

CONTENTS

ACKNOWLEDGEMENTS

Table for Eight and *Commando* appeared originally in *The New Yorker*; *Over the Side* appeared in a collection of stories, *A Map of Hearts* (published by Lindsay Drummond), *I Was Monty's Double Once Removed* in a slightly different form in the *Leader* magazine, and part of *April in Paris* in *The Sketch*. I acknowledge gratefully the permission to reprint given by the editors and publishers concerned.

AUTHOR'S NOTE

THE EVIDENCE suggests that the public appetite for books about the second World War continues unsated, so it is essential, if uncommercial, to state right away that this, while dealing with events between 1939 and 1945, is not really a book about the war. It is hoped that this disclaimer will obviate misconceptions, disappointments, angry letters from connoisseurs of global strategy, and demands for money back.

The other word I would like to get in before someone else says it is that most of this book is basically trivial. These are simply things that happened to happen to me—or happened to come to my knowledge and to interest me—during a curious period of my life a long time ago. During the war, in fact.

I would not like it to be thought that I have been brooding on this collection for the fifteen years since the war ended. Until quite recently I had never thought about it. It did not exist even as one of those lazy, one-day-I'll-get-around-to-it projects that are the permanent furniture of any writer's mind. Then an extraordinary thing happened. A French literary agent, with whom I had had some amiable dealings, wrote and asked me if I had ever thought of writing my 'war memories'. What puzzled me as much as why he should think I had any particular and marketable 'war memories' was why he should raise the matter at such a late date. The air at the time was thick with the missiles and boomerangs of statesmen's and soldiers' memoirs, the latter being never below the rank of general.

But I solved this puzzle: the agent had seen my name in

connection with a book and a film which dealt loosely with the story I have included here under the title *I Was Monty's Double Once Removed*. He must have imagined that I had a score of other war experiences on the same high level of strategic significance. I hadn't and I told him so. With Gallic *politesse* he replied that anyhow he thought I should apply my mind to those 'war memories' he insisted I must have.

The belatedness of this stimulus was its strength. It made me realise that there is a generation—I nearly wrote 'growing up' but dammit they're grown up and one is meeting them and employing them—to whom World War II is as much history as was Kitchener or Siegfried Sassoon or Mademoiselle from Armentières to me at their age. It is entirely beyond their experience or recollection. Anybody over forty now has surely been asked what the war was like, or what it was like to be bombed, or what it was like to be in the Army (Navy or Air Force) in those far-off days.

The range of the book in time and experience is from my joining the Army in London to my demobilisation in London six years later. More than half of the pieces deal with incidents while I was London-based; even when a story goes to Scotland or Paris or Rheims I was still a soldier with a desk in London who happened to be doing an out-of-town job; I was never less than an entire country behind the front line. The other items travel no farther than the English counties.

Being a soldier in London had its oddity as an experience. I remember walking homeward up Bond Street in the early hours of a morning when German raiders were overhead. Irrational as I know it to be, I was never able to duck for shelter, simply because I was in uniform. A mental picture, if nothing else, deterred me: it was of a major in a famous regiment elbowing women and children to get down into an Underground station. I was as terrified as the next man, but pride, true, false, or sinful, stood in my way and I did nothing about it.

There was nobody about that night; it was fine and the moon was bright. Some distance up Bond Street there was then an emergency water tank where a building had been bombed. Beyond it was unexpectedly revealed the façade of some of the shops in the Burlington Arcade. The vista was elegantly pretty, almost ethereally unreal; like a sketch for a painting by Rex Whistler, I remember thinking. I leaned on the brick wall bounding the tank and gazed at the moonlight playing on the black water and stippling the broken line of buildings beyond. Here, I thought, is a summary of the fantasy of this period in London: admiring the moon on a placid lake in Bond Street, with bombs coming down. Twenty years from now will anybody believe this? Even if they do, will one ever be able to conjure such a scene for them? The same applies to many things that happened to me and, often far more intensely and dramatically, to many other people.

This then is a series of loosely related, uncomprehensive, unheroic items about what we were like then and the sort of things that happened to us and around us. So, I tell myself happily, there may be two distinct publics to find interest or entertainment in what follows—that to which these are grandfather's tales told around the fire on a winter night when the television has broken down, and that which can identify itself with the period and recall events reported, sniffing again the atmosphere of the time (which cannot really be described) and finding parallels in their own experience.

I don't believe this book should or could sensibly have been published earlier. To have come out amid the crop of personal combat experiences and high-level refightings of battles from the desert to the Cabinet Room would have been to show up as a minnow among whales. Perhaps, squeakily justifying my emergence now, I might say *Après le deluge, moi.*

I

THE DAY IT ALL BEGAN

NOBODY I know was born on September 3, 1939, but it has never been suggested, to my knowledge, that that fine Sunday produced anything other than the normal, average crop of babies. I find it irrationally astonishing to realise that they have now come of age, are enfranchised, entitled to sign contracts, can sue and be sued, and that many of them are doubtless married, have babies of their own, and may even be divorced. Without exaggeratedly claiming that it seems only yesterday, I can nevertheless say truthfully that the personal details of that week-end are as clear in my memory as though it were one year ago rather than twenty-one.

I suppose most people in the building I then lived in, on the Chelsea Embankment, had their windows open, so when I was awakened by a loud radio voice it was not because any one neighbour was blasting but because everybody but me was tuned in to the same BBC wavelength, waiting for the nine o'clock news.

I had gone to bed about three, unwilling but exhausted, yet on waking there was, for once, no moment of orientation, of wondering what time—or day—it was. I jumped out of bed, ran through to the sitting room, and switched on my radio in time to hear that the Prime Minister, Neville Chamberlain, was going to speak at eleven. I had no doubt that he was going to declare war on Germany, yet it was impossible not to hope that he wouldn't; a hope without reason —no more than the wishful instinct of a peaceful man to hope that somehow there wasn't going to be a war in two hours' time.

I went into the kitchen and put the kettle on and walked around the rooms in my pyjamas, aimless and restless. The sun was streaming in and it was obviously going to be another beautiful day. I stood by the window and stared out at the familiar view. Below, the trees on the Embankment stood like a dwarf hedge between me and the Thames, with Battersea Park a neat frieze beyond. New to the scene but already familiar, the barrage balloons glinted silver in the sun and swayed a little, lazy and placid. I counted seventy of them in the wide arc of visible sky.

I went back to the kitchen and made tea and toast and ate an apple (I was a bachelor, living alone, and Sunday was my housekeeper's day off). I carried the tray into the sitting room and remembered about the papers. Usually the first thing I did on Sunday morning was to fetch them, but today I had forgotten.

Being a Sunday newspaper man I always bought the whole crop and went through them with professional care. The floor behind the front door seemed to be ankle deep in newsprint. I had been in the office till after 2 a.m., so there was little new to me on the front pages. From habit I opened my own paper at my own weekly column. It looked old and remote and irrelevant. I didn't read it.

The clock over the fireplace showed it was only a quarter to ten. I wondered if Johnny and Anthony were awake. I went to the desk and dialled Johnny's number. He was out, the maid said. He had gone over to Mr Pelissier's flat in the same block.

The three of us had met the night before and made a plan; the moment war was declared it would go into action.

John Mills was (and is) an actor. He had been having the success of his life when the threat of war closed down the run of the play ('Of Mice and Men') he was in. Anthony Pelissier was then a film script writer. Somebody told me that these two had arranged to join a certain Army unit together in the event of war and all day Saturday I had been trying to contact them. But Johnny's number was not in the telephone book and the one in *Who's Who in the Theatre* was out of date. A friendly operator in my office tried everything but failed.

About eight o'clock I went out to dinner. Normally I dined in Fleet Street on Saturdays, but now I felt like a change. I took a taxi to the Savoy Grill and chose a table facing a glass partition through which I could see the lobby entrance to the grillroom. I could not have said what I was watching for. I had given up hope of contacting Johnny in time and I was trying to think of something else. Then he walked in. I ran out and saw him disappear into the men's washroom. Anthony was with him. I cornered them and asked about their plan. Yes, it was all fixed. Yes, they thought I could probably get in too.

They joined me for dinner, and with selfconscious bravado we drank champagne. I guessed that they too had a slight feeling of 'We who are about to die', but we all behaved as if we never had a meal without champagne. Johnny explained that they had heard there were some vacancies in an anti-aircraft unit. Its advantages could be enumerated thus: (1) anti-aircraft gunnery would be very important in a modern war and it ought to be interesting; (2) the great thing, everybody agreed, was to avoid the Poor Bloody Infantry we had heard so much about from World War I; (3) the headquarters of this unit were in a London suburb, and that would be a good way to break ourselves into Army life, rather than going off to the wilds straight away; (4) it was an officer-producing unit. None of us was sure what this meant but it sounded promising.

The plan was simple. The moment war came we would

make contact with one another at once and go out to the regimental headquarters in Johnny's car.

After dinner I had to go back to the office. I wondered whether to tell the editor that if war should be declared over the week-end I wouldn't be back. But it seemed relatively unimportant, so I said nothing. A story was going round the office that some sort of compromise was going to be patched up. Mussolini had been on the telephone to Hitler for hours and war was going to be averted. It seemed to me, I recall, that 'averted' was hardly the word, considering what had been going on in Poland for two days already. The Mussolini story was passed around without elation and although nobody said he disbelieved it few showed much confidence in it. There was one man who took it seriously, though, for he went about the editorial room muttering 'Another Munich. Another Munich', in a voice of doom. He was not of military age.

About midnight I could have gone home, but I hung around for a while. The diplomatic correspondent was hanging about too. He had written his story, but had to remain on tap for developments. He knew he would get no sleep. I sat with him in a corner, smoking and talking and drinking tea. He had joined the Barrage Balloon service in 1938 and I seized on the slender connection between this and anti-aircraft gunnery, asking a string of questions about how the balloons worked. On the whole, I decided I was glad to be going into gunnery. The balloon job struck me the same way as did the possibility of being a war correspondent. If I was going to be in a war I wanted to have something to fire. Around two o'clock I found myself tired and bored with tension and went home.

The time between waking and the eleven o'clock broadcast by the Prime Minister passed very slowly. I bathed, shaved, and dressed, with the doors open and the radio playing. I wondered what to wear for joining the Army.

Nothing seemed right. In the end I put on the grey flannel suit and sports shirt I would have worn anyhow, and a pair of comfortable old shoes.

I wondered if I should write a note to my housekeeper telling her where I had gone and giving her instructions about closing the flat and storing the furniture. I wondered what I would be doing now if I were married. Probably the same, but with a good deal more talk, and much more misgiving about the future. I remember feeling unreasonably irritable and depressed.

When Chamberlain came on the air I listened only long enough to know war was declared. As I left the flat I wondered when I would see it again. Should I have packed a bag to take with me? How *did* one join the Army? (Absurdly, the phrase 'taking the King's shilling' came into my mind, with its picture of the Recruiting Sergeant and 'You're a likely lad' and all that. I wasn't a likely lad at all; I was a twenty-eight-year-old, slightly dyspeptic newspaper man—ridiculous casting.) But it was too late now. Either one joined now or waited to be called up; and that I knew I couldn't do. I slammed the door.

The Irish porter was standing in the sun at the front door of the building. He grinned and said, 'Well, here we go, sir' in a cheerful voice. I asked him to call a taxi. In the street it was warm and quiet. A few people were walking, pushing perambulators, or holding children by the hand. It looked like a perfectly normal Sunday morning.

At the traffic lights by Chelsea Barracks the taxi stopped. The old Cockney cabby pushed open the glass slide behind his head and said, 'Wot's that, sir?'

'What's what?'

'Listen.'

Very faintly I heard the wail of a siren. I had heard the sound only a couple of times before, in ARP practices.

'Is it?' said the cabby.

'Yes,' I said. 'It is.'

'Wot do we do now, sir. Go on or turn back?'

Afterwards I was ashamed when I thought of it but I said, 'Go back.'

The porter was out on the pavement now, shouting to everybody in sight to come inside and shelter. Our air raid shelter was merely a basement room, the windows of which we, the tenants, had sandbagged a couple of days before when we felt that some action parallel with the volunteer trench-digging in St James's Park was called for.

I went downstairs and found the shelter crowded. There were one or two tenants I knew by sight, one couple in dressing gowns. A man, sitting in a corner staring in front of him with red eyes, was obviously in a half-coma of hangover. The rest were people the porter had invited in from the street. There were several babies and two dogs. The porter was happily shepherding more people down the stairs. Hating crowds, I stood in the passage outside the shelter.

The porter appeared again and called out, 'Has everybody turned off their gas at the main?' I realised I hadn't, and went back up to my flat. As I turned the key I recalled with a smile that only a quarter of an hour ago I had wondered melodramatically when I would see the flat again. Inside I realised I had no idea where the gas main tap was. I rummaged around in the kitchen and found it at last. I had just got back to the basement when the all clear sounded.

In the crowd in the lobby I met my housekeeper. It seemed intolerably touching that she had come on her day off. I told her I was off to join the Army (how absurdly romantic it sounded!), and gave her brief instructions. There were tears in her eyes. Suddenly I remembered to give her a week's pay in advance.

Money. That was another thing I hadn't thought about. I looked in my wallet. To my surprise, there were more than

16

twenty pounds in single notes. Then I remembered that by chance the previous day a friend had given me the money to give to another friend to whom he owed it. I decided to send a cheque and use the cash as my war capital.

By now all the taxis had vanished. I walked along to the rank by the Chelsea Royal Hospital; I wondered how the veterans felt about the outbreak of yet another war, the second for which most of them would be too old.

Because the air raid warning had delayed me I stopped at a telephone box and called Johnny's number again. The maid said they had just left. I swore, feeling thwarted, and wondered if they had thought my failure to arrive meant I had changed my mind.

Two taxis refused to undertake the long drive out to the recruiting depot in the suburbs. A third took me on condition I gave a lift part of the way to a woman the driver was talking to as I came up. I never discovered why he was concerned to get her a free ride.

In about half an hour we reached what I thought must be the right place—a new-looking drill hall of red brick, dating, I imagined, from the Territorial Army expansion period of 1938. There was nobody about. I went inside. A Sergeant-Major with a waxed moustache was standing inside the entrance. I said I wanted to enlist.

'Regular or Territorial?' he snapped.

I had no idea. I stammered something about having two friends who must have arrived just before me. Contemptuously (or so it seemed to the recruit) the Sergeant-Major said that would be the Territorials and showed me into a room.

An officer was bustling about. He was about forty, red-faced, with a fierce Kaiser Wilhelm moustache I couldn't take my eyes off. I told my story again and the officer said Johnny and Anthony had just left. He had enlisted them and sent them home for razors and spare socks. They were due

17

back by four o'clock and he suggested I should follow the same plan.

He then led the way into another room where some women in khaki (ATS, I learned later) were sitting behind bare wooden tables). Facing all but one of them were empty chairs. Facing the remaining one sat a young man with cropped hair and no tie. He looked uncomfortable and fiddled with his cap under the edge of the table. The girl opposite him was asking questions and filling in a form.

The officer set me down in a chair facing another of the girls, who sat with her pen poised efficiently and began to ask brisk questions. Name, address, date of birth, place of birth . . . when I said 'Glasgow' she asked what county that was in. I couldn't remember whether Glasgow was a county in itself or was included in Lanarkshire. I said Lanarkshire and she seemed satisfied.

'Religion?'

'Presbyterian.'

From long practice in printers' composing rooms I was following her writing upside down on the form and noticed that the space for religion was a very narrow column. Her pen hesitated.

'C. of E. (Church of England) would do for that, wouldn't it?' she asked, a doubt in her voice.

Mildly I said I didn't think so.

'Oh, I know,' she said brightly, 'I'll put Meth, for Methodist.'

'But I'm not a Methodist,' I said stubbornly. 'I'm a Presbyterian.'

She frowned. I murmured that I didn't feel like making an issue of it.

'Better be C. of E. then,' she said judicially; 'that's the most usual. There's no abbreviation for Presbyterian.'

I had an idea. 'Couldn't you put C. of S.?' I said

helpfully. 'You see the Presbyterian Church *is* the Church of Scotland.'

The girl shook her head firmly. I began to see myself condemned to non-combatancy for want of an abbreviation.

'Or P-R-E-S,' I suggested.

That did it. She could just get four letters into the column. I felt I had been saved from a technical apostasy.

After a few more questions the girl handed the form across the table and pointed with her pen to a closely-printed omnibus question.

'Just see if anything there affects you.'

There seemed to be a little embarrassment in her tone.

I studied the question. It demanded whether or not I suffered or had ever suffered from a series of ailments. One of them, and probably the reason why she didn't feel equal to reading the question aloud, asked bluntly: 'Are you a bed-wetter?'

I handed the form back and said the answer was no.

With the completed form in my hand I went back to the officer's room. The Kaiser-moustached officer took a Bible from under some papers on his desk, put it into my hand and, looking at me fiercely, went through the process of attestation. I had never before heard the words of the oath. The officer declaimed them in a loud, dramatic tone. My reaction was to respond in much the same tone. So we stood toe to toe shouting into each other's faces. Far from finding the situation comic, I was oddly moved. I undertook with passionate sincerity and determination to defend His Majesty's person. When the officer finished I had a lump in my throat.

'Right,' said Kaiser briskly. 'Now off you go and get back as quick as you can with your shaving kit. Where do you live?'

'Chelsea,' I said rather apologetically.

19

The officer scowled. 'Long way,' he said. 'How are you going to get there?'

I said I had a taxi waiting outside.

'Good show,' said Kaiser, his brow clearing.

Until that moment I had forgotten about the taxi. It was turning out to be an expensive business, joining the Army.

A Medical Officer came in and looked at me quickly. I was relieved, if not wholly convinced, that my physical perfection was so apparent. It struck me later that his examination would not have discovered, for instance, a wooden leg.

As I came out into the sun I noticed there was a pub opposite. I had never needed a drink more. Now that the step was taken reaction was setting in. I ran across the road just as the door was closed. It was two o'clock, Sunday closing time in the London area.

Back at my flat again I took the long-suffering taxi-driver upstairs and we had a drink while I packed. I telephoned Johnny's flat once more. He had left a message. They were lunching at the Savoy. By the time I was ready to go the taxi-driver was sitting back on the sofa, studying the sunlight in his whisky. He looked thoughtful. I was about to suggest moving when he looked up and spoke.

'Well, sir,' he said with decision. 'You're my last fare.'

'How's that?'

'I'm going to turn my cab over to the fire service. I've been thinking about it. They want cabs and they want men. So I'll join too. I was in the last show and I'm going to get into this one, somewhere. Suppose I keep on the road. What'll happen? Petrol'll get scarcer and scarcer. Cabs'll make less and less. And then in the end there won't be a living in it. Better make the break now than later.'

He finished his whisky and got up with the air of a man whose mind is made up and finds it a relief. I guessed he still had to explain his decision to his wife and this had really been a rehearsal.

By the time we reached the Savoy the grillroom was empty but for Johnny's table. There was a very young officer there, a friend of Johnny's, and we three recruits took childish pleasure in embarrassing him by practising saying 'Sir'. It was a high-spirited luncheon party. When the bill came John tore it up on the principle that he had spent so much money in the restaurant in his time that it was only right the management should celebrate his joining the Army.

'Send it to me—and try and find me,' he said to the waiter as he handed him the torn scraps of paper. The waiter grinned happily, for he had his tip.

When we got back to the headquarters a large, sealed envelope was awaiting us, addressed to the Officer Commanding —th Bn., Royal Engineers, at Royston, in Hertfordshire, about thirty miles from London. The Kaiser-ish officer glared at us and barked, 'Who's the senior man?' We looked at one another foolishly. The officer decided on Johnny, as he had been sworn in first.

'You are in charge of this party,' he said. 'Understand? You are responsible for the others and for the papers.' He thrust the envelope into Johnny's hand.

Outside Johnny showed immediate if light-hearted qualities of leadership, of which delegation is the first principle.

'Watts,' he said fiercely, mimicking the officer, 'you are in charge of the papers. Understand?' And he thrust the envelope at me. 'Pelissier, you are in charge of the route. You will navigate. Understand?'

'The papers' became the stock joke of the day. The words had a cloak-and-dagger sound that pleased us. If we weren't on a vital military mission at least we could play-act that we were. The papers must go through.

Before long we had a very unmilitary difference of opinion about the route. Eventually we arrived in Bedford, about twenty miles on the wrong side of our destination.

21

The town hall clock was striking six. We went into an hotel as the King's speech began to come over the air. While we had a late tea we looked around the thick-carpeted comfort of the lounge. It was an average out-of-town hotel, but at this moment it seemed all the luxury we were leaving behind, the last stop before the barrack room and—so First-War-minded were we—the trenches. I realised I was a little scared of what the next hour would bring. We found our road and estimated we would be at the camp in about half an hour. But freedom was becoming precious. We remembered that the pubs opened at seven so we stopped in a village and waited. But after one drink we were impatient to get on and get it over.

At last we came to a few huts in a wired-off field, just short of a village. There was a tent at the gate and by it stood the smallest, wispiest soldier I have ever seen. He carried a cane under his arm and wore a red band on his arm with the letters RP (Regimental Police). Anthony looked at the encampment with distaste.

'This can't be it,' he said, but there was no confidence in his voice. We sat in the car and stared in silence for a moment. Then I got out, clutching 'the papers'.

'Do you think that troglodyte is our comrade-in-arms?' Anthony murmured. (We later found that as all the able-bodied men were required for work and there was little policing to be done a handful of shrimp-sized weaklings had been made RPs temporarily. Such was the influence of Anthony's personality that the whole camp was calling them troglodytes in a couple of days.)

The troglodyte wasn't at all sure about three civilians, one with a sealed letter for the Commanding Officer which he wouldn't let out of his hands. But at least we established that this was, in fact, our destination.

We were conducted to the company office and somewhat reluctantly I handed over 'the papers' to a Sergeant-Major.

Johnny and the Sergeant-Major stared at each other for a moment and then recognition dawned. The Sergeant-Major, then a corporal, had been Johnny's driver during the making of an army film in which he had appeared.

A soldier-clerk took us outside and directed us to a marquee to get beds for ourselves. We had our coats off and were stuffing straw into palliasses, when a soldier came in. He was a stern-faced little man with tight, pale lips and greying hair. He took off his tunic and went to work among some stores on the other side of the marquee. On the tunic he threw down I noticed three stripes, a brass grenade and a crown. I didn't know exactly what it all signified, but obviously this was some superior kind of sergeant.

Anthony glanced towards the newcomer but apparently overlooked the tunic.

'What kind of a dump is this?' he asked. Anthony has a crisp voice and his manner can be abrupt. 'How's promotion? How long does it take to get a commission?'

I tried to signal, indicating the rank-emblazoned tunic. It was no good. The Company Quartermaster Sergeant told us tersely that he was not there to answer recruits' impertinent questions. (Anthony had quite a lot of minor troubles with the CQMS after that.) By the time we had dumped our palliasses in the hut allocated to us the supper call sounded.

There was stew for supper. We ate from borrowed metal plates which tasted of metal polish. Back in the hut we started to write out a list of things-to-buy-tomorrow. Enamelled plate, knife, fork, spoon, and mug were the first items. In the hut were two other recruits, silent, glum-looking youths, self-consciously busy settling in. There was no furniture of any kind. A fat young man with a black moustache and a foot in plaster limped in. He had recognised Johnny from the stage and screen. He invited the three of us to go across to a hut opposite, occupied by the dispatch riders. They were very hospitable, and we drank

23

gassy beer from bottles. Somebody played an accordion (which I learned to call a squeeze-box) and everybody sang. I learned the words of 'Nellie Dean' and the time passed quickly.

Before going to bed we strolled down the lines and had a last cigarette in Johnny's car, parked at the far end of the field. Already it looked embarrassingly opulent and out of place. The desire for privacy was making itself felt, but also there was something we wanted to discuss. The conversation in the DRs hut had completed a process begun when we were sent off from the recruiting headquarters. We now realised that three out of the four points on which we had based our enlistment had proved wrong. (1) We were not in anti-aircraft gunnery. This was a searchlight unit. (2) The 'London suburb' idea had been quickly dispelled. Already we were marooned in a field thirty miles away. (3) It was certainly not an officer-producing unit.

The only point on which we were right so far was that we had, at least, avoided the Poor Bloody Infantry.

We went to bed—or lay down on our amateurishly filled bags of straw. I wished I were fatter. There seemed no position in which my well-defined hipbones were not trying to dig into the unyielding floorboards. But I fell asleep at last.

A siren woke me. It was three o'clock in the morning and bright moonlight filled the hut. We were ordered to get dressed and double to the slit trenches between the huts. We had not yet mastered the military art of dressing quickly. By the time we got out the trench beside the hut was full. I jumped down recklessly on top of some men who pushed me around and swore sleepily at me. I swore back. Anthony followed. When we looked up, Johnny was standing on the parapet, floodlit by the moon. He was dressed with an actor's precision and looked incongruously well-groomed.

'I suppose,' he said, 'I just stand here and die like a gentleman.' The trench laughed and made room for him. Johnny's popularity had begun.

24

Next morning we were detailed for a fatigue squad and issued with denim overalls. We went out in a truck to a quarry to fill sandbags. We shovelled diligently and were very tired by supper time. We had had no time to buy plates, but now we did not notice the metal polish flavour.

That night the Sergeant-Major sent for us.

'Commissions,' said Anthony, as we scrambled to tidy up. 'There's been a mistake and now they're going to send us away to train to be officers.'

'Why?' said Johnny gloomily. 'What the hell do we know about anything? Why should we be officers?' He was tired and felt low, and I was with him. We felt sure the war would go on for ever and we would never be anything but private soldiers.

The Sergeant-Major told us he had decided that as from tomorrow morning we three would be the Company Commander's runners. We would divide the twenty-four hours into three shifts of eight hours each, working out our own schedule. The important point was that there must always be a runner on duty at the dugout where the telephone was.

As we turned to go the Sergeant-Major picked up a khaki greatcoat and threw it to Johnny.

'Here, better take this for the man who's on at nights. It gets a bit parky. You can share it till you get your uniforms.'

Back in our own hut we felt better. We had at least a bit of uniform. And a job. We were in the Army now.

Johnny settled down to clean the tarnished buttons of the common greatcoat. Anthony began to rearrange, in the light of experience, the straw in his palliasse. I started to write a letter to my editor, in lieu of notice. Suddenly I realised I would not have been missed yet. It was Monday night and the Sunday newspaper week begins on Tuesday. It was only thirty-six hours since I had hoped there wasn't going to be a war.

2

POP GOES THE DIESEL

In the Indian summer of 1939 there was plenty of time for recruits in the searchlight division of the Royal Engineers to loaf, gossip, and brood. The training was infantile: if you were assigned, as I was, to be a Listener you stood with earphones on and your eyes on the ground while a buzzer was run up and down a wire strung like a clothes-line and on a word of command pointed to where you believed the sound to be coming from. I had explained that I had unbalanced hearing—one ear perfect and the other about ten per cent—so that sounds coming from the right made more impression on my left ear than on the other. The chances of my locating a source of sound accurately were almost nil, except by calculation so elaborate as to be little better than wild guesswork.

But nobody in authority paid any attention, and there were other jobs in the nine-man searchlight team that I dreaded more—such as operating the lamp or the diesel-engine generator which I knew to be far beyond my technical capacity.

However I have a way of achieving what I want by a slow relentless process which I like to think of as determination or pertinacity but which I recognise could equally well be called nagging. It has been known to move members of my family to whom it has been applied to a state approaching hysteria. I decided I was going to be a Spotter, because that meant sitting in a swivel chair in the field and gazing at the sky in search of enemy aircraft, and then, by a series of

26

codified vocal signals, directing the hand-operated search-light beam. I can't remember how, but I became a Spotter and many a pleasant afternoon I spent drowsing in my swivel chair.

This was—though the phrase had not then been coined—the phoney war period and while searchlight teams of which I was a member illuminated many a friendly plane we saw nothing of the enemy. Sometimes the aircraft we chased with our beam had been sent up for us to practise on, but sometimes they were more actively employed planes whose pilots were infuriated, and rightly, by being enveloped in the glare of searchlights in apprentice hands when they were trying to get home to their base.

We learned to take apart and reassemble a Lewis gun (of course, by the time I came to more active soldiering the Lewis gun had disappeared and I had to learn all over again) and we did fatigues. Most of us were old enough and sophisticated enough to detect which were real jobs that had to be done and which were invented by the NCOs to keep us busy, and we soon had our avoiding devices. The simplest was simulated keenness. When a sergeant came to the door of a hut and roared 'Sapper' you dropped whatever you were doing and ran at him. He never chose the first man but picked some laggard for the job. I fell in with an old soldier, not old in years but in experience and guile, who taught me such simple but valuable tricks as never walking across the camp empty-handed. If your objective was merely the back of the Mess hut where you planned to sit in the sun for a while and have a cigarette you grabbed an empty pail or a plank of wood and marched purposefully. The empty-handed strollers always caught the chores.

In the first few weeks we were not allowed beyond the gates of our field and after work we simply loafed. My theatrical friends Mills and Pelissier invented a number of childish games to pass the time. One was a dialogue with our children (none of us had any) about what we did in the war. It went something like this:

'What did you do in the war, daddy?'

'I was in the Army.'

'What regiment?'

'Not regiment. Corps. The Royal Engineers.'

'Oh, did you build bridges, and dig tunnels and blow up things?'

'Well, no, it was anti-aircraft.'

'How many German planes did you shoot down?'

'Well, you see, it wasn't quite like that. We had search-lights . . .'

'Oh, you lit up enemy planes for the fighters and gunners to shoot down?'

'That's right.'

'How many enemy planes did you light up?'

'Well, actually, where we were . . . I mean *while* we were there . . . enemy planes never . . .'

'Did *you* swing those great big beams about in the sky?'

'No, you see there was a team . . .'

'What did *you* do?'

'Well, I listened.'

'You what?'

'Listened. Listened for the sound of enemy planes. . . .'

'Couldn't you have done that without being in the Army?'

The only thing we were sure of was that if our war continued as now any such future conversation must end in humiliation and loss of face in the eyes of our young.

Non-active Army life brings out the schoolboy in any man, I think. Johnny Mills had recently played an Old Vic season and when we were detailed to be the Company Commander's runners he and Pelissier invented a brilliant *ad lib* routine by which one delivered a message to the other in various theatrical styles. The Company Commander, a portly, humourless stockbroker, came round the corner of the telephone dugout one day in time to see Mills drop on one knee in front of Pelissier and declaim: 'Sire, o'er yonder hill a Messerschmitt doth dip its silver wing. . . .' It was embarrassing all round.

We had a lot to learn about the officer–man relationship. In the hands of regular officers we would have had a rough time, but our officers were Territorials and not very sure on protocol themselves, as well as being harassed by finding themselves suddenly full-time soldiers in a less than organised army. When we were queueing for our uniform issue, for all the world like a straggling column of crowd players reporting to Wardrobe, Johnny took his pile of clothing, topped by a steel helmet, and said to the officer supervising, 'Do you think it'll run?'

Pelissier went on parade one day in a pair of boots he had bought for himself. The Quartermaster (whom he had accidentally antagonised on arrival) spotted them and barked, 'You—why are you wearing those boots and not the issue?' I suppose it was the actor in Anthony that caused him to reply in precisely the same offensive tone, 'Because they're more comfortable.'

In my own case, simple ignorance was the cause of my gaffes. At my first kit inspection I was, naturally, asked why certain articles were missing. I replied that I had given them away as I had no use for them and other men seemed to have. Similarly it seemed a good idea to me when I remembered that my brother-in-law in Yorkshire knew a number of mill-owners and I wrote to him for some khaki material which we had made into much more satisfactory trousers than those issued. When these were noticed and the truth told I think the Sergeant-Major was too flabbergasted to react normally and no action was taken. Equally innocently I asked an officer to cash a cheque—and he did. And once when an MO sought to down-grade me from medical category A1 because of some minor ailment I was annoyed and asked if I could have a second opinion. I didn't get it but I was not down-graded.

When it appeared that intensive aerial attack was not imminent—and searchlights are not much use in daylight anyhow—we were allowed to leave camp from five till seven o'clock each evening. This was a release of an importance it is hard to appreciate unless you have been in a bath-less field for several weeks, sleeping on the floor and eating Army food cooked by amateurs.

In the village there was a hotel with which the three of us at once entered into an arrangement to provide us with the three things we wanted as we had never wanted them before —baths, decent food, and drink—in the limited time of our daily freedom. It worked very efficiently. By 5.10 we were in a hotel bathroom. One bathed while two shaved—we were not too fussy about changing *all* the water each time— and we were downstairs by 5.30. On the bar stood three large dry martinis.

This was the relaxation peak of the day. Apart from our clothes, there was for once nothing to differentiate this moment from civilian, civilised life. Another round of martinis and it was about six, when we trooped into the dining room where three plates of bacon, eggs, tomatoes, and fried bread awaited us. And eventually, clean and replete, we strolled back in good time to camp.

Sometimes we had time in hand. Once when a friend sent me, most inappropriately for a private soldier in camp, a bottle of Kummel and we were drinking it in the hall of the hotel, one of our officers came by. We shot to our feet; he smiled and said, 'Carry on', but without stopping to think I said, still stiffly at attention, 'Would you like a glass of Kummel, sir?' He was so astonished he accepted, but he drank it rather quickly and I always thought afterwards that he was especially stern with us to compensate for his lapse.

The economics of this way of life were, of course, ridiculous. As sappers we were paid two shillings a day, which paid for exactly one martini—although that seems wonderfully cheap now. Johnny, by far the richest of us, was our banker, for while Anthony and I had to make arrangements to draw money from the local branches of our banks, and then try to get there during banking hours, Johnny had a Post Office savings account, a relic of his days as a touring actor. It was a great convenience. Time after time he would draw the maximum three pounds and hand us each one, making our above-income life possible again. We knew this camp life couldn't last and we were prepared to make inroads on capital so long as a few small relative luxuries were available.

It came to an end abruptly. One Sunday afternoon we were told to pack our gear and in an hour we were in a truck, destination unknown. Truck riding, by the way, is a trick that has to be acquired. Ten men in a fifteen-hundred-weight Bedford have to stand where they can and clutch the nearest iron strut over which the canvas roof is fitted. Crossing fields in this way can make equilibrium a struggle. On this trip Johnny was thrown on his back by a sudden lurch. Sprawling among our feet, immobilised by knapsack, gasproof cape and respirator, he looked up unsmiling and murmured, 'It's the only way to travel.'

The field we were deposited in had a row of nice, solid-looking brick buildings along one end. It seemed a reasonable place by our new, humble standards. But it was not for us. It was the home of a pack of foxhounds. We had a single Nissen hut with a lean-to for cookhouse. Our first job was digging a latrine trench.

But we were on detachment; out of the recruit stage, on our own; practically, as we saw it, in action.

Our detachment commander was an amiable enough man, a big corporal with a handsome black moustache. He looked intensely military, the very type of the dashing young captain; it was disappointing to find he was a motor-car salesman, flashy, work-shy, a show-off when officers were around, a liar and scrounger. From the start he was sycophantic to Johnny, as a film star—very embarrassing for Johnny—and blusteringly inconsistent with the rest of us. He committed the unpardonable Army crime of borrowing money from the men under his command, though, of course, we did not know how unpardonable this was and merely thought him ill-advised and something of a nuisance.

But he was amiable and easy-going most of the time and as we were young (to the Army at least) and keen we did our jobs and maintained a curiously high degree of largely self-imposed discipline. I, an inveterate organiser and list-maker, worked out the rosters of duties, including guards, so that there was no wrangling or injustice over that, and the Corporal was content. We grated less on one another than a handful of men in an isolated field might be expected to. There was, of course, the Bore, the dirty man, the artful dodger—the types you will find, it seems, in even the smallest random group of men, but by a system of plain speaking and majority rule we managed.

The Bore was memorable only because he introduced a new phrase to me. He was an engineer with technical and theoretical training and he loved to use the textbook's words, especially when he found the rest of us ignorant of them. One night we were discussing some small and probably elementary technical point of searchlights which one of us (almost certainly I) had trouble in understanding when the Bore butted in.

'It's the initial inertia,' he said.

'The what?'

'Initial inertia.' He waited smugly for us to ask him to elucidate, and we did. He had a glorious time with the ensuing monologue. I don't remember much of it, but I can still hear his cockney voice constantly coming back to 'initial inertia', a lovely phrase which, said by him, seemed to be awash with 'sh' sounds. It has to be a simple example of a technical matter to stick in my mind and all I remember is that initial inertia is represented, for example, by the moment in the swing of a pendulum when, before starting the return swing, it is halted for a split second by its own weight.

Years later I was in a club when somebody remarked on the barometric clock behind the bar. 'I thought there was no such thing as perpetual motion,' he said. 'There it is.'

'No, it isn't,' I said, and the Bore himself was never smugger. 'It isn't, because of initial inertia. That's why there *is* no such thing as perpetual motion.'

Being the sort of club I would be a member of, there was nobody to contradict me; indeed I earned a lasting, if local, reputation for erudition.

Soon the recruit camp life was a nostalgic memory. There was now no night without guard duty—two hours on and four off—and usually the detachment was turned out once or twice in the night either on an alert or for practice. By military standards, our days began late—breakfast was at eight—but one never seemed to have an unbroken sleep of reasonable length.

The days were filled with work, genuine work now, for in addition to the camp chores there was a programme of maintenance. The diesel generator had to be cleaned, polished, and painted, and so had the lamp. Paths had to be made, weapon pits dug, and revetments built and turfed for camouflage. Our hands were soon calloused from pick and shovel—no, that is not quite accurate in my case. The first time the Corporal saw me wield a pick he said, 'Have you ever used one of these before?' I said I hadn't. He watched me for a moment longer, then said, 'I think you'd better have a shovel.' I saw his point; I believe there is a phrase in

33

military manuals about situations where a soldier becomes a danger to his comrades.

I had to take a good deal of teasing at this time because of my braces. With all this strenuous exercise I broke my Army pair irreparably and wrote to my shirtmaker for a new pair, mentioning that if possible they should be khaki. They were, but what I had not allowed for was that the shirtmaker had made them exactly like the non-khaki ones I had had from him before, and they bore an elegantly embroidered monogram. The first time I took off my tunic there were some incredulous looks and then the teasing began.

As the Army slowly became better organised somebody realised that we outpost soldiers had never done any rifle drill. We had two rifles in the detachment but they were solely for the use of sentries. One day the Corporal was ordered to send three men into headquarters for a drill parade, and Johnny, Anthony, and I were detailed. The lorry which conveyed us was late, so we had to fall in hurriedly as the last file of three. I was in the rear rank with Johnny immediately in front of me. In a moment of dead silence a radio began to play from a hut where the dispatch riders lived. It was a record programme and the announcer's voice, loud and clear, proclaimed that the next item would be 'Little White Room', sung by Frances Day and John Mills. There was something eerie about standing to attention as a private soldier on parade with the voice of the soldier in front of you floating out across the field in song—and rather a coy song at that. A titter, immediately hushed by the Sergeant-Major, ran through the ranks. Johnny stared rigidly in front of him but I watched the back of his neck gradually turn red.

When the drill was over we found we were mutually amazed that we had got through it—sloping, trailing, porting, and presenting our arms if not faultlessly at least pass-

34

ably. We each had our reason. Johnny had played a soldier in a film, Anthony had spent one unwilling term in the OTC at Charterhouse, and I had been in the Boys' Brigade in Glasgow at a time when that Christian organisation still carried dummy rifles.

Shortly after this we were moved on to another site—and the rain came. The new site was on a hilltop, and more remote than ever. Whoever laid it out had slipped up. The hut was more than the regulation distance from the lamp, and although we had been moved intact as a detachment we had changed our commander and instead of the Corporal we had a lance-sergeant who was a stickler for the book. We were never formally inspected while on this site, but the Sergeant dutifully indented for a bell tent and set it up closer to the searchlight. Thus while we used the hut by day we had to plod out through the rain and mud every night and sleep in the tent. We were none of us expert campers and I don't think I was ever really dry in the next few weeks.

The diesel on a searchlight site had to be 300 yards from the lamp so that the noise would not interfere with listening, and on this site it was parked down a narrow track which was never less than six inches deep in mud. The diesel had to have a separate sentry at night and it was his task to start up the engine every hour to keep it warm. This particular diesel (they all had personalities, mostly villainous) was a sulky brute. For those less technically well informed than I, though I find it difficult to believe there is such a person, it should be explained that a diesel engine is wound by a crank to create compression and that if the decompressor bar is struck at the right moment the engine will start. The trick is to find the right moment; if you miss, you have to start the heavy winding all over again. Clad in respirator and steel helmet, armed with a rifle which you were trying to keep dry under a waterproof cape, the task of starting this diesel was formidable. One night I found the answer. If you sang or hummed the old nursery tune 'Pop Goes the Weasel', in rhythm with your winding, the timing was just right to make this recalcitrant machine combust. I tried it several times, and it always worked:

> *Half a pound of tuppeny rice*
> *Half a pound of treacle*
> *That's the way the money goes*
> *POP goes the diesel*

On the POP you hit the bar.

You felt a fool doing it, on a rain-lashed hillside in the middle of the night, trying to keep your footing in the mud, but it worked. I got on the field telephone to Johnny, the sentry at the other end, and told him my great discovery. The three of us must have saved dozens of man-hours and much exertion, and I was absurdly proud of my discovery.

Perhaps because of my singing those absurd lines to Johnny over the telephone we developed the habit of passing the time by singing to one another. (Thank heaven a field telephone is unlikely to be tapped.) We played two games— remembering old songs or making up ribald parodies of popular ones. Johnny, who came up as an actor via musical comedy, sings extremely well and he also has a wonderful memory, so I had the best of these programmes. I would wind the handle on the box and when Johnny answered would say, 'What was the thing Fred Astaire sang in "Hit the Deck"?' And usually Johnny would come back with 'You mean . . .' and go straight into the number.

Then, abruptly again, this phase came to an end. One day Johnny and Anthony were summoned to Battalion Head-quarters. Commissions! The one word leapt to all our minds. But why had I been left out? I could think of a number of reasons but preferred not to. The others were polite enough to be sympathetic in the midst of their excitement.

When they came back they had long faces. Commissions had never been mentioned, but the CO had asked them to form a battalion concert party. There were advantages to be gained: they would live in a proper house (sleep in a proper bed!) at HQ and they would be free of the grim routine of detachment life. But they had put up a case for including me, and had been turned down. I did not mind this. Their qualifications were impeccable: Johnny could sing, dance, play the piano, act, and was an experienced man of the theatre; Anthony had acted too, written and directed for the theatre, and the stage was in his blood. They were professionals; I would have been a passenger. A concert party hardly needs the services of one whose connection with the theatre has been as a critic.

It would be foolish to pretend, even in retrospect, that I was in anything but very low spirits when their truck bumped out of the field and faded from sight.

Relief, or at least change, was not long in coming. The tempo of life on searchlights was slow and monotonous but when things happened they happened fast. I was hailed one afternoon by the usual Sergeant's shout across the field and within an hour I was at company headquarters reading a manual on how to be a Detachment Commander; a few days later I was an acting temporary corporal, and posted.

The Sergeant-Major kindly told me that I must not be nervous of taking command, especially as he had taken care to post me to a detachment of men I wouldn't know, and consequently they wouldn't know that this was my first command or that my stripes were so newly tacked on my sleeve. I had no worry about commanding men but I was disconcerted when I walked into the hut at my new site and three or four of the men sitting at dinner looked up and said, 'Hi, Steve.' We had been recruits together.

37

The detachment was in a deplorable state of slackness and unless I wanted to run the risk of losing my stripes as quickly as I had gained them something had to be done. I knew I would be accused, though not to my face, of 'playing soldiers' or 'throwing my weight about' but there was no alternative.

Without realising it, I took the most unpopular step first, so the worst was over quickly. I instituted, from the day after I arrived, an 8.30 a.m. parade. They had never been paraded; apparently they had just got up in the morning and drifted off to their various jobs when they were ready. From the buttons of the tunics I saw hanging up I felt sure none of them had worn anything but fatigue denims for weeks at least. They were outraged at being made to clean their buttons, put on tunics and caps, wash their gumboots, and form up in line at a fixed time. When I asked a couple of them when they last shaved they rapped out the stock answer, 'Last night when I came off guard, Corporal. Blade's blunt and you can't get any here.' When I presented them each with a blade of my own and packed them off to shave my unpopularity probably reached its peak.

But as always happens in such cases they took to the new ways quickly and began to take a pride in their appearance. Before long—without instructions—some of them were boning and polishing their chin straps.

The diesel on this site was tucked away in a cosy hollow and there was a bell tent adjacent, which I presumed to be sensibly provided for the sentry's shelter from the prevailing rain. Stupidly, when I made my rounds I inspected the diesel without looking into the tent. On the third night I walked down to the diesel about midnight before turning in and I couldn't find the sentry. It was a fine night and there was no reason for him to be in the tent. I shone my torch in and there he was, asleep on a roughly-made bed of wood and canvas. On the ground beside him lay his rifle, steel helmet, and respirator.

I picked up these and went back to the hut and woke the next sentry due to go on. He grumbled sleepily but went off, and in due course the tent-sleeper came in. But I pretended to be asleep, having put his equipment under my bed. In the morning he looked at me curiously. He was a big, strong-faced man named Job, and his expression was a mixture of sheepishness and smouldering truculence. When I dismissed the parade I told him to stand fast. To my surprise another sapper, McDonald, stood fast too. I was playing all this by ear and at that moment I was nonplussed. McDonald spoke. 'I made the bed, Corporal,' he said. I stood them at ease and walked away.

I invented some task in the hut but I could feel the curiosity—almost tension—in the whole detachment. The other men were going about their work but they were watching to see what was going to happen next. Job and McDonald were standing staring in front of them. I let five or ten minutes go by then I went back and marched them off to a far corner of the field. I guessed that this was a partnership and it was no guess that they were the two tough guys of the detachment. They were obviously wondering what I was going to do next, and so was I.

It all seems terribly trivial now but I might be with these men for months to come in this isolated life, and unless some understanding was reached, it was going to be intolerable. I dismissed them but added, 'Don't go away. I want to talk to you.' I then simply said that if we were going to live and work together they would have to accept that I was in charge and that I expected them to do their duties properly. The incident of the night before was never mentioned specifically. Later that day the pair of them brought the bed up from the tent and chopped it, rather ostentatiously, into firewood for the cook.

Job, I discovered, had been a regular soldier and he fully realised the enormity of a sentry being found asleep at his post. What I was not sure about, and I had nobody to consult, was whether my not putting him on a charge would be regarded as a sign of weakness. But no; Job took it as an act of mercy and we became good friends, even though I later had to send him before the Colonel for being absent and he went to the Glasshouse for fourteen days. When he returned he was asked if he wanted a fresh posting and I was flattered that he declined and came back to me.

Job and McDonald had been petty—sometimes, I think, not so petty—part-time criminals and both had been in prison more than once. McDonald told me over cocoa late one night that he had come out just before the war began. He cursed himself for the folly that had earned him that particular stretch. He had been out of work, which I gathered was not unusual, and he filled in the time with a minor racket which consisted of selling packets of washing powder from door to door. The packets, in fact, contained French chalk. The trick was never to go to the same house twice. In case this should happen he always carried in his pocket the butt end of a stick of shaving soap. If the housewife recognised him from his first visit and berated him for selling her stuff that wouldn't lather he would apologise profusely, explain that occasionally a dud packet turned up, and offer her a demonstration. Then he would dig his nails into the shaving soap, ask her for a basin of water and produce a fine foam. But on this occasion he went back *again* by accident to a woman he had visited twice before and she locked him in and called the police.

One of Job's favourite tricks was to get a job driving a coal lorry and, by an ingenious system he had devised, he would load two or three more bags than normal capacity. The money for these was his profit and the result nearly doubled his wages. Once when I arranged leave for him

40

when it was difficult he was so grateful that he volunteered to do me a favour. I said it was unnecessary, but he insisted. He took a piece of paper and drew a map to show me where he had once dumped a cash box in the Thames while being chased. I don't know if it was true, but there was no doubt about his sincere desire to do me a favour.

Both men were devoted girl-chasers and living in the same hut with them it was impossible to avoid knowing that they had various girl friends in the village.

As their time out was very limited, and always in the afternoon, I couldn't see how they saw much of them. But before long I found out. There was a tent at the gate of the field and this served as a kind of sentry box for the man who patrolled the field at night. I noticed Job and McDonald slipping off from time to time, but it was no crime to go and talk to the sentry when nothing was happening. Then something I overheard made me investigate. One night I walked up to the tent about ten minutes after Job had vanished. The sentry was patrolling the other side of the field and did not see me in time to give a warning. Job was literally in the hay —or at least straw—with a girl. I ordered him back to the hut, ignored the girl, and walked away.

Later that night Job sought me out alone and said, 'Sorry about that, Corporal, but I wasn't doing any harm.' I said mildly that we couldn't have girls on an operational military site. Also I didn't want any trouble with the village people. 'But it's quite safe with her,' said Job earnestly; 'she's married—and she's pregnant.'

Anybody who has commanded men in even the most humble capacity knows that popularity must never be courted, but it is often a puzzle to discover why at a particular time or with a particular man one is obviously popular or unpopular. At one point I could not think why the formidable Job, who could do practically everything except read and write better than I could, was regarding me

41

with what was clearly admiration. I couldn't ask, but neither could I find a reason. Batches of recruits in training were sometimes sent out to us for practical instruction in the working of a searchlight site. Job was my diesel man, and a first-class mechanic. My technique with these trainees was so simple and instinctive that I had never even thought about it. I took them to the diesel, making sure Job was on hand, gave them a brief, general description of the function of a generator, and then said (probably with a studied glance at my watch as if I had an important duty elsewhere), 'Now have a good look and if you have any questions ask Sapper Job here. He's the best man at his job in the battalion. There's nothing he doesn't know about diesels.' And I walked swiftly away. It came out one day that Job, who knew that my practical knowledge of the diesel engine went no further than how to start it, thought this was the cleverest trick he had ever come across. 'No wonder you got promoted,' he said one day in a burst of confidence.

The combination in Job's character of two strong traits—the practical and the unscrupulous—made him about as useful a man as you could wish to have around, provided you were prepared to keep one eye almost permanently closed. Once when we were doing one of those tiresome navvying jobs which were so frequently called for it was necessary to shift quantities of gravel to a distant point in the field. At first we used buckets and any sort of bags we could find, but clearly what we needed was something the Army didn't issue—a wheelbarrow. The matter was not so much discussed as merely mentioned. Next day Job was pushing a wheelbarrow. It had been newly and rather crudely painted. I asked where it came from.

'Borrowed it,' said Job, neither pausing nor looking at me.

Later I inspected it more closely. The letters 'CCC' were just discernible under the paint. I had no doubt what they meant—Cambridgeshire County Council—but I greatly

42

doubted if the civil powers were co-operating to that extent. I said nothing and when the job was done the barrow disappeared.

When Christmas came near there were rumours of a special dinner at headquarters, but I guessed they were no more than rumours because it would mean leaving the searchlights virtually unmanned. Then I discovered that the 'dinner' was in fact to be a special ration issue—of pork. It did not sound very exciting, so I wondered what I could do, in the interests of morale, to make Christmas a little more festive. I mentioned this to our officer the next time he came round and he agreed. He took me into Cambridge in his car to see what we could buy. But we had left it rather late and stocks were low. All we could find that seemed at all suitable were very large turkeys, too big for most families. However we bought one, weighing twenty-eight pounds.

When I returned to the site the ration lorry, which included the postal delivery, had called, and there was a large wicker hamper for me. A kind friend had sent me one of those Christmas collections of everything from plum pudding to stem ginger and crystallised fruits. But the principal item was a turkey—weighing twenty pounds. So now we had forty-eight pounds of turkey for ten men and—I suddenly realised—nowhere to cook them. All our cooking was done on the regulation Soyer stove, a U-shaped affair of iron, not unlike a smallish family boiler. Job dealt with the problem almost as soon as it was put to him. He went off and found a quantity of clay, turned the Soyer on its side, enclosed it in clay, improvised a door out of a biscuit tin lid, propped the contraption up to allow for a fire underneath and, behold—an oven.

We had our gargantuan Christmas dinner and for several days afterwards anybody was free to stroll into the kitchen at any time and have a snack of cold turkey in his fingers.

Although my little band of non-combative warriors paraded properly dressed as soldiers every morning they immediately changed into working clothes. There was an 11 a.m. break and a woman in a cottage across the field used to serve them with tea and buns. It was on the perimeter of the site, so there was no objection to their going there. One morning a large car drew up at the gate of the field and what seemed to me a dazzle of officers stepped out. I had at this point met nobody above the rank of major, but these were led by what I recognised to be a major-general, in breeches and shining field boots. I reported myself and he identified himself as my Divisional Commander.

"Just passing, Corporal," he said, "and thought I'd like to look round. I don't often get a chance to see a site, and you chaps don't have many visitors, do you?"

He glanced round the field. There was not a soul in sight. He looked understandably surprised and I was just about to explain when from the door of the cottage a couple of hundred yards away issued the most unmilitary and—if the circumstances had been different—comical file of men I have ever seen. Every one was wearing a bulging, shapeless Army issue pullover, collarless shirt, denim trousers stuffed into gumboots, and a Balaclava rolled up to make a ridiculous little round woollen cap. To make it worse, they were in single file, slouching through the mud, and as they approached (knowing that they shouldn't salute without proper headgear) they hung their heads and trailed self-consciously by in silence. Except that there were eight of them they looked like a battered version of Disney's Seven Dwarfs. And this the first time I had been called upon to exhibit my detachment for a senior officer! Instinctively I almost ordered them to fall in, but an unhappily clear picture of how absurd—and shaming—they would look lined up stopped the words in my throat. Instead I found myself saying rather gruffly, 'Morning break during maintenance

44

period, sir.' The General said gravely, 'Yes, of course,' and changed the subject.

That night a notice went up on the hut door. 'During morning break any man leaving the vicinity of the hut will wear tunic and cap.' They had decided long since that I was a fussy character, so they just shrugged and mumbled a bit and humoured my whim, but no general ever came to see us again.

Not long afterwards John Mills, by then a sergeant, asked to be released from the concert party and to serve in a capacity which could lead to a commission. He was duly sent to a site as detachment commander. The first night, sitting around the hut, the men started to talk about their previous detachment commander. They told, *inter alia*, about the morning parades and having to put on a tunic and cap to go for a cup of char.

'He was all right,' one of them said, 'but he could be a proper bastard.'

'What was his name?' Johnny asked.

'Corporal Watts,' he was told.

Loyally he tried to tell them that I was an old friend of his and that I was not at all a bastard, but he doesn't think he made much impression.

3

A WAIST ON THE BEAM

CHANCE RATHER than skill or any irresistible aptitude as a leader of men had made me a Lance-Sergeant within four months of joining the Army. This proud, romantic title has nothing to do with any weapon borne by the holder. A Lance-Sergeant is one grade below a full Sergeant (though he is always addressed as 'Sergeant'), and in the Royal Engineers he wears the three chevrons on his sleeve, which makes him look like a full-fledged sergeant in most other regiments. But the full sergeant of the Sappers adds the brass symbol of a bursting grenade in the V of the stripes.

The chance which favoured me was the arrival of a new Company Commander, bringing with him his own nucleus of officers. They had been drafted in for the specific task of shaking up this Territorial company and the new Major's first decision was to weed out the NCOs in charge of detachments and replace them with new, freshly-trained men of his own choice. In this reshuffle I moved up from Corporal, went through a short refresher course, put up my third stripe, and was duly posted. I was unlucky enough to be assigned to a detachment on whose site the junior officer and full Sergeant responsible for a group of lights were also housed. Unlucky, because one of the attractions of being a DC was that with any luck one ruled supreme in one's own little isolated domain.

The officer was a mild, competent man (of all things, a plant pathologist in civilian life) who did not interfere much.

The Sergeant was a friendly man with formidable technical qualifications. But before long he was promoted to Mechanist Quartermaster and moved on to higher and more technical things. So Sergeant Hicks arrived.

It was apparent from the start that Hicks was an unusual type to find in a searchlight unit entirely composed of nonprofessional soldiers. Even his appearance was different. He was a short, straight man, with cropped grey hair and a back that arched inward to a tiny waist. He had obviously had his tunic altered (those were pre-battledress days) so that it curved in to a skin-tight fit and looked like a Victorian corset. Physically, he was a model of soldierly deportment.

Before long I knew his whole history. He told it promptly and repeatedly. He was at pains that everyone should know he was not as we others were. He had been twenty-seven years in a famous cavalry regiment. His gods were horses and polish. For him the Army had gone to pieces when it lost its horses, but the fragments might be held together if redoubled emphasis were laid on polishing. A searchlight he obviously regarded as a rather silly toy from the functional point of view, but its extensive metal and glass surfaces attracted him as objects for polishing.

He had retired from the Army a few years before the war and become a commissionaire, opening taxi doors outside a London hotel. (Several men I knew swore to comb the hotels of London after the war until they found Sergeant Hicks and then spend whole days arriving and leaving just to make Hicks open doors for them. They proposed to tip in coins of the smallest known denomination and if possible report him to the management for insubordination.) As soon as he was out of the regular army he joined the Territorials, and the unit nearest his home happened to be this searchlight battalion. I imagine he found it unbearable to be totally divorced from the Army, but there was an ungenerous story that he had joined because he was short of

47

beer money one Thursday night and the Territorials paid half-a-crown on joining.

I first met Hicks when the officer sent for me and introduced us. Hicks' sharp little brown eyes fastened on my sleeve, with its new white chevrons of rank, and when we left the officer's hut and walked across the field he asked, with a poor attempt at casualness, how long I had been in the Army.

'Four months.'

Hicks grunted and I knew what he meant. I was sympathetic; that we should be a bare fraction of a rank apart, that we should both be called 'Sergeant', was a deep-wounding insult to those twenty-seven years of service.

After midday dinner that first day Hicks summoned me and bade me accompany him on a tour of the tiny camp. He hardly spoke as we walked round, but his face warned me, and when we completed the circuit he announced, with a wealth of adjectives, that, taking a pigsty as the model of hygiene and cleanliness, my detachment compared unfavourably.

The next few weeks were trying. In my civilian way, I figured that my primary duty was to maintain and operate a searchlight for the illumination of enemy aircraft. Sergeant Hicks took a different view. He would take my men away from work and maintenance on the light and the diesel and put them to polishing their metal eating plates and the cook's buckets. He would call kit inspections which were not intended to check the completeness or serviceability of the men's official belongings but turned out to be instructional demonstrations of how a kit should be laid out symmetrically; the blade of the knife must face the right; the spare shirt must be rolled to show one button, not two; the hair-brush must come before the boot brush as you looked at the kit. Only a bloody fool would put them the other way round.

When Hicks saw the list of daily duties pasted on the hut door he demanded to know why there were no periods allocated to interior economy. I had never heard the phrase at that time. All it meant, apparently, was cleaning out the hut. He asked when the floor had last been dry-scrubbed with brick-dust. I had never heard of any such process. He found a soldier's boots on which the studs on the sole were rusted. He hurled the boots into a corner and dispatched the offending soldier to fetch *his*—Hicks'—boots from the shelf above his bed. When they arrived the men gaped to see the studs burnished and shining. I noticed that the eyelets through which the laces were drawn had been scraped and polished and the leather laces themselves blacked and polished.

I had a miserable time, but my men had worse. The sheer pointlessness of what they were made to do, while living in a muddy field and losing a lot of sleep on night duty, produced in them a sullen mood, and somehow—because I could not join them in denouncing Hicks—they blamed me as at least a party to this hideous regime.

When Hicks did show any interest in the searchlight equipment it was only to give orders that the brass on the lamp (non-working parts) was to be 'highly-polished' (pronounced as one word) or that the tyres on the wheels of the mobile generator were to be painted with black enamel. But if the sapper who operated the lamp came on parade with his hands showing signs that he had been working with the carbons which made the light he was shouted at for being filthy and given some punitive duty such as polishing the outside of a dixie which a few minutes later, in the course of its natural duties, would be smoke-blackened on the cooking stove.

Almost daily I pointed out that necessary duties were delayed or neglected by these decorative activities, but I was told to mind my own business and thank God my

49

detachment had come under the saving influence of a proper soldier before it was too late.

Sergeant Hicks never admitted his technical ignorance, and this, I decided, more than any other factor put the men against him. Each man had a job, partly or wholly technical, and Sergeant Hicks posed as knowing more about each than the man himself. I recognised in this a face-preserving attitude common among professional soldiers. If you don't know—bluff it out. Never let the man know you don't know, otherwise you cannot hold his respect. That is the theory.

But when your soldier is a motor mechanic or an electrician, doing in uniform a job closely approximating to his civilian trade, the theory is liable not to work. Bluffing about a man's own trade (which is not yours) is perhaps the quickest way to *lose* his respect.

One day the Company Commander paid the detachment a visit. It was dusk and the men were at action stations. I was busy with my megaphone directing the team in manipulating the beam on to an imaginary aircraft. Sergeant Hicks' was a purely administrative job. In action he had no function. But, of course, on this occasion he was conspicuous, marching smartly round the site at the Major's heels. Eventually they took up a position on a knoll at the far end of the field and watched the detachment in action. We had had a lot of practice and as a team were good. But that night the beam was not at its best. It was wavering and, though there were no clouds to deflect it, it was spreading out towards the top in a diffusion which would weaken its effect. The lamp operator was a technician and he knew without being told what was wrong. From where I stood I could see the silhouette of the operator, busy about his lamp, peering into it with his dark-glass frame to shield his eyes from the many-million-candle-power glare. The crackle and sputter of a new carbon burning itself in were faintly audible and I knew all would be well as soon as was humanly possible. But on the knoll the Company Commander must have said something. Suddenly Sergeant Hicks' voice roared across the dark field.

'Get a waist on your beam,' he yelled.

Now the ideal shape for a properly focused searchlight is like a pencil for about seven-eights of its length, and then there should be a slight but distinct indentation. I am not sufficiently technical to explain why this should be, but I knew that when the beam was right it had this neat 'waist', as it was called. There was not a great deal of jargon in the searchlight game in those days, but 'a waist on the beam' was a common phrase, just as a 'beard' or 'trousers' on it meant ragged, blurred edges instead of the clean, sharply-defined lines which denoted correct focus.

Sergeant Hicks was obviously parroting what the Major had said. I did not acknowledge the shout, and a few seconds later the beam settled into the desired shape, complete with waist.

In the hut afterwards I heard the lamp operator murmur to his pal, 'D'you hear that? Little bastard. "Get a waist on your beam." What the hell does he know about it? Next thing he'll be telling us to climb up it and polish it.'

A little later Sergeant Hicks came into the hut. 'What kind of a bloody detachment do you call this, Sergeant?' he bawled. 'Putting up a beam like that. No waist on it—till I told you.'

I said nothing. Hicks was angry and excited. I did not feel like apologising and I didn't want a row in front of the men.

But the next night I realised that Sergeant Hicks had got hold of something he wasn't going to let go. He nosed about the lamp. Whenever it was switched on he talked about the waist. He played with the phrase as with a new toy. He felt he had now put the finishing touch to his

51

technical knowledge. I looked at the operator and knew there was murder in the heart of that conscientious technician. The awful, moronic repetition produced a fury inside me too and I could not trust myself to speak.

Not long after this there was a case of meningitis in a neighbouring detachment and all the others in the vicinity were quarantined. Our rations, even water in cans, were thrown over the hedge to us. The gate of the field was padlocked and a yellow flag flown over it. We went on with our normal duties for about a week and then the lamp broke down. All the skill and experience of the operator could not make it work. The men, who were beginning to show signs of strain under the monotonous confinement, cheered up at once. They knew that in the ordinary way I would have put in a report by telephone and a Mechanist Quartermaster would have come out. But now, with nobody allowed to enter the field, they welcomed the prospect of a few days' inaction. Even if it meant more polishing, at least they would get an uninterrupted night's sleep, a real luxury in searchlight life.

When Sergeant Hicks heard the lamp had broken down he cursed loudly and strode out across the field to where the operator was still vainly tinkering with the mechanism. He pushed the man aside and began to finger the wiring beside the main switch. After a moment he stepped back and pushed the switch lever home. The light went on. The operator's face was dark with rage. Later he told me that just as the Sergeant pushed him aside he thought he had found the fault and was about to try the switch. But it was no good saying that now. The Sergeant had repaired the light when everybody else had failed. He had saved the detachment. Almost he had won the anti-aircraft war. He was unendurable.

That afternoon a signal came that the quarantine was lifted. The Sergeant went off to the village by himself and I gave my men a couple of hours off duty in relays. They went off in pairs down to the village and forgot the too familiar field and Sergeant Hicks in the simple joys of a bath and a pint of beer. By eleven o'clock they were all back and at their posts. The beam was perfectly focused and we were in the midst of a routine practice when I heard the voice of Sergeant Hicks. I did not know until that moment that he had come back; I should have, as the pubs had closed.

'Get a waist on your beam,' he roared. 'Get a waist on your beam, you——'

He was drunk. His voice came nearer in the dark, shouting this same phrase over and over again, varying only the expletives, and these not much. Sometimes he shouted clearly, sometimes it was just an inarticulate, half-gargled bellow. Suddenly he lurched into the pool of moving light thrown down by the beam. His cap was on the back of his head and his eyes were bloodshot. A straggle of short grey hairs lay matted on his brow. His tunic buttons were undone.

'Get a waist on your beam,' he yelled in my face, not even looking at the beam, which was perfectly focused. 'I know you hate me, you little civvy bastard. You all hate me.' He threw his arm out in a comprehensive gesture and almost lost his balance. 'Get a—waist on your—beam.' It was louder than ever, as if to reassert himself after that momentary loss of control. He came still closer to me and dropped his voice. 'I know you hate me. Because you don't like having a good soldier around. *Sergeant*'—he spluttered his contempt—'What a bloody Sergeant. H'much service? Four bloody months. Four bloody minutes it looks more like. If you're a Sergeant I'm a——' It would have gone on indefinitely but at that moment a quiet voice came from behind us.

'Sergeant, go to bed,' said the mild, competent officer.

53

Twenty-seven years in the cavalry were more powerful than alcohol.

'Suh,' barked Sergeant Hicks. He saluted unsteadily and vanished into the darkness.

The men were frankly jubilant. After they had doused the light, fallen out and gone to bed, I could hear their chuckling talk in the dark and the unmistakable sound of voices mimicking a drunk saying, 'Get a waist on your beam.'

In the morning the cook had just brought in the big dixie of tea when the Sergeant burst into the hut. He was in crumpled shirt and trousers and it was obvious he had slept in them. His hair was rumpled and there was grey stubble on his face. He had never been seen unshaven before.

In one hand, at arm's length, he carried a gumboot. Everybody in searchlights had a pair of gumboots for quick dressing when there were night alarms, and they were kept under the beds.

'When I find the bastard who . . .' the Sergeant shouted.

The inside of the boot was sopping wet. We all knew what had happened. But usually drunks were cunning enough to use other people's boots. He stormed for a moment and then went out.

We never saw him again. The driver of the ration lorry told us later that he had driven the Sergeant into Company HQ, and had last seen him nervously fingering his buttons and straightening his cap outside the Major's hut, the hollow back more tautly concave than ever.

That night I made my usual round of the sentries. One of the men on duty slept in Sergeant Hicks' hut, indeed his bed was next to the Sergeant's. I was fairly certain the guess I had made was right but I could not resist checking up.

'About that affair of Sergeant Hicks' boot last night,' I said. 'Did you . . . ?'

I could not see the man's face in the dark. There was a

second's hesitation and then he said, 'Well, Sergeant. If I may say so, I've met his kind before, Sergeant. Drunks, I mean. I knew what would happen. So I just put my boots under his bed and his under mine. I didn't see why . . .' His voice was rising in self-defence.

'Quite,' I said and walked away.

Next morning a new Sergeant arrived. He was a stern, taciturn man, and a firm disciplinarian. He knew a lot about soldiering, but he also knew a lot about searchlights, and about men. He was probably surprised by his own quick popularity.

4

OVER THE SIDE

THE RATION lorry was late. For the last half-hour I had
been glancing across the field towards the gate, then glancing
at my watch, irritated and ready to curse the driver when he
arrived, although both he and I would be well aware that it
was not his fault. Being cursed when he was late was just
part of the driver's job. What the driver would never know
was that my irritation was really self-criticism, because I
was nervous and it was absurd that I should be. But as a
sergeant in charge of a searchlight detachment I never grew
out of being nervous when new men were coming. In the
strange, isolated life we led one personality in our tiny com-
munity of ten, living in one small hut, could make all the
difference.

The lorry had still not arrived when the cook banged a
dustbin lid with a ladle and uttered a snarling yell which
would have been translated only by an expert as 'Come and
get it'. We sat down to the inevitable stew at the scrubbed-
white table in the hut—only eight of us for we were below
strength through sickness and I was awaiting two replace-
ments. Before we had finished the spotted dog and custard
the lorry came bumping across the grass and stopped outside the lean-to cookhouse. I went out, swore briefly and
perfunctorily at the driver, and looked curiously at the two
men who had jumped down from the back of the truck and
now stood looking lost with their kitbags and blanket rolls
at their feet. Two of my sappers, who had left the dinner
table without being told, helped the driver and the cook as

they unloaded the rations. I ran a now-practised eye over the boxes and bins as they came off the lorry, noting that the emery cloth I had been requisitioning for days had at last arrived and that the meat, for once, was worth roasting to make a change from the eternal stew. Then I went over to the two new men.

'What names?'

'Johnstone 24, Sahnt,' said one, a thin, sharp-looking fellow of about thirty. I liked the prompt way he came to attention and rapped out his name, adding the last two figures of his Army number to identify himself from other Johnstones in the battalion.

'Benson, Sergeant.' The other soldier spoke slowly and I was surprised to notice he blushed as he spoke. He was very young, and obviously shy; looked a bit goofy, too, I thought. Still, he looked strong and there was probably no vice in him. Yokel, probably. Slow but sure. As a pair the newcomers seemed decent enough. I was relieved.

'Right,' I said with the conventional NCO brisk authority which now came naturally. 'Get your stuff inside. You'll see the two vacant bunks. Just unpack your knife-fork-spoon and see what the cook's got left. You can unpack after dinner. It's not a bad dump this—bit lonely, but we don't grumble and you're not expected to. I'll talk to you later about what jobs you're going to do. Both been on detachment before?'

'Yes, Sahnt.'

'Yes, Sergeant.'

'Okay. Get going.'

At the end of a week I had forgotten Johnstone 24 was new; but Benson was a bit of a problem. Well, to be accurate, he was only half a problem. The other half was West, who had been with me for a couple of months by now. He was a man you had to watch, but he was no real problem before Benson arrived.

57

It was like this: everybody on the detachment had realised straight away that Benson was on the goofy side. Nobody said or did anything about it, except that I would hear someone mutter when he had gone out of the hut, 'Jeez what a dope that Benson is.' But it was said amiably, mildly.

It was a simple enough case. Benson was eighteen. He had been in a county regiment of infantry until his battalion had gone to France and then he and a few others had been left behind as too young. These 'immatures', as they were called, were transferred to anti-aircraft for home service. Benson, who was quite communicative about himself when questioned, had worked on his grandfather's farm since he was fourteen. He slept in a loft, worked from dawn till dusk, and was paid 5s. a week, all found. That came to light on the first pay day when somebody remarked that it wasn't worth queueing up for 10s. and he wished he could tell the Army what they could do with their measly money. Benson thought it was wonderful to get 10s. every Friday with a bit more going into your credit all the time. Similarly, when somebody moaned about the beds—canvas nailed taut on rough wood frames—Benson frankly revealed that it was the most comfortable bed he had ever had. He thought the food was wonderful too. In short Benson was that rare soldier who found Army life more comfortable and profitable than the world from which he had come.

West came back from leave a couple of days after Benson and Johnstone 24 arrived. When he heard Benson make one of his simple, sincere remarks his sharp Cockney voice was raised at once. I was sitting on my bunk in the corner, writing a letter, but something in West's tone warned me a problem was taking shape.

'Geh,' said West. 'Y're kiddin'. Wod'ya take us for—coming that Boy Scout stuff.'

Their surprise was mutual; they looked at each other, each trying to decide if the other was mocking him. West unable to believe that anybody was so dumb as to like the Army; Benson incredulous that West did not believe him or share his enthusiasm. West made up his mind first.

'Strite, chum, eh? You think this is the bleedin' life, eh? Cor . . .'

From then on Benson was an unending source of amusement to West, so fascinating he could not let him alone.

West was a wide boy. He'd tell you that himself. He was proud of being wide. I gathered he had been a minor gangster in a London suburb. I had heard him describe with relish the larks he had got up to as a schoolboy; they were neither more nor less than petty crime. He had been in a reform school. He had been in gaol. He had been abroad as a ship's stoker when he was on the run from the police. And now he was only twenty-one. But the balance of his account showed a sufficient profit of easy money as against steady work, of freedom and evasion as against detection and punishment, to qualify him as a wide boy, despising work and workers, proud of his knowledge of how wrestling matches were fixed and how you could get in on certs at the dogs if you knew the right people; even how you could 'make' an overcoat by seeing to it that if you had to go to gaol in the winter for a few weeks you were picked up coatless so that the benevolent authorities would issue you with one on release and you could flog it for ten bob the first hour you were out.

West was a volunteer—and a good soldier. My guess was that his joining the Army had coincided with a period when he was on the run and he had probably thought he could get out again when the heat died down. I had been just long enough in the Army myself to know that West's type tends to soldier well. Why? Because it's the smart thing to do. Wide boys don't go about bashing their heads against brick walls. They either walk carefully round the end or they climb over, using all the right footholds.

59

If I had been a sergeant in a normal unit, living in a proper camp or barracks, I might have been taken in by West. But in the constant close contact of this isolated life I inevitably learned more. I heard the grumbles, the remarks when they forgot I was there or thought I was asleep.

West was an arch-grumbler. He was forever telling the others what a bloody life this was, how it contrasted with his gay independence in civvy street, how the Army should be run—what he'd do when this lot was over. But he was on the job like a flash when the alarm bell rang, he moved at all times with the nimble agility of his breed, he took in instruction with an aggressive shrewdness, he adapted his self-protecting technique to the needs of soldiering in a way that was nothing sort of masterly.

Up to the time Benson arrived I thought I had West pretty well taped. For one thing I had overheard West say a score of times he was going over the side, and many a morning I had caught myself glancing at his bunk when I woke, wondering if it would be empty. But West's Army crime sheet was clean. He had sized up the relation of punishment to crime under military law and apparently decided that wide boys didn't buy a few days' freedom in London at the cost of a considerably greater number of days in the guardroom or a stretch in the Glasshouse. Crime where punishment was a certainty was no game for a wide boy.

But Benson, in his innocent way, brought a new light to bear on West for me.

One night the pair of them happened to have been on guard together and I was lying awake when they came into the hut and made themselves the mug of cocoa which every sentry had before he turned in. I cocked an ear to hear if West was still ragging Benson about his ignorance; the point was approaching where I would have to talk to West sternly

60

in private, for the other men were beginning to tire of the ceaseless, repetitive ribbing.

It was a childishly simple process which gave West his fun. He would ask Benson innocent-seeming questions about his civilian life, which the country boy would answer truthfully and naïvely. West would press his questions in such a way that Benson was made to look quite ridiculous. Benson never seemed to get wise to it. He never lost his temper or sulked. He always answered, and then if West's cackle of laughter was shriller than usual and some of the others couldn't help joining in he would look from one to the other with a baffled, slightly hurt expression, yet still with a friendly smile on his face.

But now as I listened while they stirred their cocoa it was Benson who was doing the questioning. He was asking West all about his civilian life, and West was pouring out colourful tales of his smartness and the glamorous life he had led. It was fascinating, for West had the Cockney gift of telling a story well. Benson, of course, was enthralled. Tales of adventures with the police, parties at Brighton to celebrate a successful coup, hazards overcome in luring a girl away from her current protector, who then sent some of his boys after you—I cautiously moved my head and through half-closed eyes saw Benson with his mug in both hands, held half way to his mouth, while over the rim his eyes were big with wonder.

I turned over and simulated a sleepy growl as though their voices had roused me. They whispered for a few minutes and then went to bed.

After that night I noticed a change in the relationship. Benson was eager and industrious, but slow to learn. His handling of weapons was clumsy, his rifle drill strained and uneasy, and on the diesel engine, to which I had allocated him, he got no further than turning the crank handle with more enthusiastic strength than anybody else. But now I

61

noticed that Benson was taking instruction in his off-duty time, with West as instructor. They would stroll off up the field together between tea and the dusk stand-to and I could see the two figures bent over the side of the diesel. One day I came into the hut and found them poring over a map, West explaining in unorthodox but vivid language what the symbols stood for and how the contour lines worked. Next time Benson was on guard I noticed his handling of his rifle had improved a hundred per cent. I could not resist glancing at the inside of his beautifully blanco-ed rifle sling. The side that did not show was dirty—a typical West trick.

Now there was much less teasing. Occasionally round the supper table West would make a crack at Benson's expense, but there was no more to it than the unending rivalry of the townsman and the countryman and they exchanged friendly grins with the joke.

For a while I thought the problem had solved itself. West was unchanged except in his attitude to Benson; he was still smart, cocky, selfish, unprincipled, and efficient with a rather spurious dash about it. Benson had become more proficient but he was still on the slow side. Then I began to notice something new. At roll-call one morning Benson, whose slow rather self-conscious response of 'Sergeant', pronouncing all the letters, had grown familiar to my ear, suddenly snapped out a harsh, nasal 'Sahnt' which might have been an echo of West. I glanced up to make sure it was Benson who had answered. Then one Saturday night Benson came back from the village drunk and was sick in the night. Next morning I took him aside. He was shamefaced and sorry; he had only had two pints of beer but somehow it hadn't agreed with him. Was he used to drinking beer? Yes. Had he ever drunk as much as two pints in one evening before? Oh, yes. The way he said it, I knew he hadn't.

But West's influence continued to grow. At the times

62

when I wasn't supposed to be listening, I often heard Benson grumble; the same sort of growling, empty, I'll-show-the-bastards sort of grumble West indulged in. There was nothing I could do about it. Technically, Benson's soldiering had improved. If a man jumped to a word of command quicker than before you could hardly tick him off for it merely because he was imitating another man.

Then Benson's first leave fell due. According to the roster posted up inside the hut door he was off after duty on the Friday. In practice after duty meant after dinner, a rule I had made so that a man had a chance of catching a hitch into the nearest town and getting a train home the same night. By dinner time Benson was ready, his haversack packed, his battledress pressed, his boots shining, his hands scrubbed red and his nails cleaned. (I often wondered why practically every soldier's idea of smartness on parade fell about twenty per cent short of his standard for going on leave.) The man who had been on leave for the previous seven days was due in on the ration lorry, but when it arrived he was not on it. He had not reported in at Headquarters. This meant Benson couldn't go. I was sorry for him. I sent for him and explained. We were down to the minimum necessary to run the light. Two men could not be spared at the same time. Benson would have to wait till the other man showed up. He looked glum, but accepted the verdict without a word.

By stand-to there was still no sign of the absentee. At supper I noticed that Benson had changed into his old battledress and his dubbined boots. Nothing was said. It rained after dark and when I came in from a round of the sentries I stopped outside the hut door to take off my mud-caked boots. Two of the men had scrubbed the hut floor that afternoon and there was a Company Commander's inspection every Saturday morning. As I leaned on the door untying my laces I heard Benson's voice inside.

63

'They can go and —— their —— Army,' he was growling. 'They're not going to —— me about like this. I've
had it. I'm going over the —— side.'
'That's the idea, chum,' came the crisp cheerful voice of
West. 'You show 'em. If it was me I'd be over the side by
now.'
Benson went on in the same vein. Every phrase, every
adjective, every intonation he had picked up from West.
There was something almost touching about the bravado of
it and I smiled to myself in the dark and made a noise with
the door handle before going in.
It was a quiet night without a call-out. When the cook
brought in the tea in the morning I sat up as usual, lit a
cigarette, coughed, decided smoking before breakfast was a
bad habit, and looked around—the daily routine. Two
bunks were empty. After daylight there was only one
sentry.
'Who's on guard?'
'West,' said the man who had come off the turn before.
'Then where's Benson?'
Nobody spoke.
'Cook,' I shouted through the open door. 'Tell West to
come and see me—at once.'
There was silence in the hut. Outside the cook's voice
could be heard yelling up the field to the diesel where the
sentry was usually to be found. A few moments elapsed
and then the cook came in.
'He ain't there, Sarge,' he said. 'Can't see him any-
where.'
I was out of bed and half dressed now. I went outside,
buttoning my tunic. The field was deserted. An idea struck
me and I walked round behind the cookhouse.
'Where's the DR's bike?' I called back to the cook.
'Round the back, Sarge. It's always there. It's——' the
cook came round the corner, saw the empty space, and

64

stopped. The dispatch rider himself had heard and he now appeared.

'It was there last night, Sergeant,' he said, anxious to defend himself.

There was a constrained air at the ablution bench and the breakfast table. There had not been a case of absence in the detachment before. Now, with the man who had failed to return from leave, we were three short, and each man saw the prospect of an extra two-hour guard, thereby losing some of his precious sleep. There would be trouble over the disappearance of the motor bike. They knew I was in a bad temper and there was a dull, depressed silence.

Just as the men were getting up from breakfast to go to work Benson walked in. He was unshaven and dirty and he hung his head.

'Where the hell've you been?' I barked at him.

He did not reply. I was thinking: I ought to put him on a charge but really he's only been absent about an hour—reveille till now. It's not worth it. Probably decided to go and then funked it. I said: 'Where's West?'

Benson looked up, a vacant look on his face. 'Don't know, Sergeant,' he said.

'You mean you and he didn't go over the side together?'

'No, Sergeant.'

It sounded like the truth.

'All right then, get yourself cleaned up and get to work. I'll deal with you later.'

When the ration truck came at midday the man who had been on leave was on it, complete with medical certificate to cover his absence. But no West. I decided to leave the case of Benson until I knew more about West. At least I was now short of only one man—no worse off than if Benson had gone on leave. Later in the day I sent in my report to Headquarters, showing West as an absentee from reveille.

Three days later a message came from HQ that West and the motor bicycle were now in custody and Sergeant Watts would report to the Company Commander next morning. I rode in on the ration truck and gave formal evidence of the discovery of the absence of West and the bike. West, standing hatless between the escorts, was rigid and expressionless. When the Company Commander asked him if he had anything to say he barked 'No, sir' without hesitation. He was remanded to the Colonel.

When West had been marched out I asked the Company Commander if I might visit the prisoner. Permission was granted.

West looked up when I walked into the hut where he was in custody, but his face showed neither surprise nor pleasure. I was curious to know what had happened, but now I didn't know where to start, what line to take.

'What did you want to do a silly thing like this for, West?' I said at last.

West said nothing.

'Tell me what the trouble was and maybe I'll be able to help you.'

'No trouble, Sahnt. I just went over the side.'

'Trouble at home?'

'No trouble, Sahnt.'

'Oh come on, West. Help yourself if you won't help me. Must have been something on your mind. Did you want to get away from the detachment? Why didn't you come to me about it?'

West's shrewd sharp eyes rested for a long moment on my face. Then he said:

'Awright, Sahnt. I'll tell you. I *did* want to get away from the detachment. I'd had a gutful, Sahnt, honest I had. It's that Benson. He's got on my nerves. Gets me down, 'e does. And, look, Sahnt, when I come out from whatever the Old Man gives me I want to get posted somewhere else. If they send me back where Benson is I'll go over the side again, so help me I will.'

You could never be sure with West if he wasn't trying something on. But this time he seemed sincere enough. An idea formed in my mind; I decided to try it.

'Why did you send him back?' I said quietly.

'Me? Send him——? Who'dya mean, Sahnt? Send who back—where?'

'Come on, West. Why did you? You know what I mean. Why did you stop Benson going away?'

'I told you, Sahnt. I went over the side because—well, what I told you, like I've often said I would. I don't know nothin' about Benson—except he's the biggest pain in the . . .'

'You mean *Benson* went over the side like you've often said *you* would. He got the idea from you—like a lot of other ideas—and he's too dumb to realise you never meant it.'

West's face broke into a cheeky, friendly grin.

'But I did it all the same, Sahnt. Didn't I?'

'But it wasn't your idea even then. That's what I'm getting at.'

'Okay, Sahnt,' West grinned. 'Whatever you say. You're the boss. Only don't bring any of this up before the Old Man, will you? I'll deny it if you do.'

'I'll see about that. But go on now you've started. I still want to know what happened.'

'How about a fag, Sahnt?'

There was a cunning smile on West's face; he knew I knew smoking was against regulations for prisoners. He was blackmailing me for my curiosity. I handed him a cigarette. I didn't take one so that I could grab West's if anybody came in. West took a long draw and then spoke slowly, the words coming out with the smoke.

'That dope Benson,' he said slowly. 'Honest, Sahnt,

67

you'd hardly credit it. I'm on sentry and he comes creeping out at first light. I thought it was the cook up a bit early. But then he comes out from behind the cookhouse pushing that bike. Him with a bike! Doesn't know enough to fall off. He pushes it across the field to the gate. I'm watching him from up by the diesel. By the time I get across he's managed to get the engine started somehow. I yell at him but he's off. I knew he wouldn't get far. Then a milk lorry comes along and I thumb a lift. Sure enough, there he is about a mile down the road—missed the turning short of the village and pushing the bike back to the crossroads. The engine's seized too. Well, Sahnt, I puts the fear of God into 'im, takes the bike away from him and sends him off back to camp, blubbing like a kid. I knew you'd hardly have had time to miss him and as like as not you wouldn't bother to put him on a charge. Especially as you'd have something more to worry about. Meaning me and the bike.'

West drew deeply at his cigarette and shook his head sadly. 'What a dope that man is. Not fit to be let out alone. He'd get on the nerves of a saint, he would.'

'And you're no saint, West, eh?'

' 'Sright, Sahnt. That's one thing even me old mother wouldn't call me.'

'You realise it was your fault Benson ever thought of going over the side?'

'Me? What did I ever do, Sahnt? See, that's what I mean. He gets you into trouble for doing nothing.'

'You know very well what I mean, West.'

'Look, Sahnt,' said West in a resigned voice. 'Let's forget we had this little chat. I'm charged with leaving my post as a sentry without permission, absenting myself without leave for three days, and being in unlawful possession of a military vehicle. I plead guilty. No explanations. They won't charge me with desertion because I gave myself up. That's all. I get twenty-eight days Glasshouse and that won't kill me. Why, I've——'

I cut in on his boast: 'Why didn't you come back with Benson? That's what I can't understand.'

'Me come back?' West's voice was shrill. 'Don't make me laugh, Sahnt. I'd have wanted my head examined if I'd done that. We'd've looked sweet and pretty, that dope and I, pushing the bike in and saying, "Please, Sahnt, we didn't mean it." ' He mimicked in an awful child voice. Then he became serious and came close to me. 'Look, Sahnt. I couldn't, honest I couldn't. I'd have brought Benson in as a naughty boy I'd caught in the act—and what would that make me? A bleedin' nark, that's what. Or else I'd have to have pretended I'd gone over the side with him—and then funked it and come back. That would make me just as big a dope as Benson. Nah, Sahnt, you can see it my way too if you try. One dope like that's enough to be ashamed of in your detachment.'

I nodded and reached for the cigarette end between his fingers. He pulled it away for one last, finger-burning drag. Then he surrendered it with a grin. Outside I threw the butt away and climbed up beside the driver of the ration lorry, who was waiting for me.

'What'll he get, Sarge?' the driver asked when we were clear of HQ.

'What he deserves,' I said without thinking but not wanting to discuss it with the driver. The trouble was he'd get a great deal more.

5

A LAND FIT FOR PIERROTS

ROSES FELL to ruin on the quiet pavements of Frinton-on-Sea in the summer of 1940. More important things were happening at the same time in other, unquiet places, such as Dunkirk, Calais, and the skies over southern England, but I saw nothing of these while I trod the carpet of petals daily as I went about my military duties.

I had arrived at Goojerat Barracks, Colchester, in April, stripped off my sergeant's stripes, fitted the white band of officer-cadetship on my forage cap, and immersed myself in the anxious business of training for a commission. The anxiety arose from two sources: I was twenty-nine years old and a long time away from school, so classroom and book learning did not come easily; on the practical side it was little better as I am not deft with my hands nor am I mechanically minded. Also the letters 'RTU' hung like a menace over our heads; they stood for Return to Unit, and a cadet who did not show sufficient aptitude, or behaved in a manner considered unbefitting an officer and gentleman, was sent back whence he came with those deadly letters on his record, thereby greatly decreasing his chance of ever being commissioned.

This was the end of the phoney war period, but the training was still greatly influenced by 1918 thinking and practice. I remember an elderly general concluding a visit to us with a pep-talk the text of which was that we should always pull our belts in one hole tighter than was comfortable for in this way we would be braced and on our toes.

This seemed to me as nonsensical then as it does now when I have reached an age when one is inclined to tell the young what is good for them.

Our closest contacts with the war were the depressing radio news we listened to at every opportunity and local aerial activity, though that affected us rather less than the civilians of the town. There was nothing martial about being turned out of our barrack rooms in the night into slit trenches except that we had to take steel helmets, respirators, rifles, and packs with us. Nothing ever happened in those raids and I invented a method of propping my feet against one side of the deep, narrow trench and my pack against the other and going to sleep suspended rather like a Dickensian chimney-sweep's boy. Sometimes there were dogfights overhead during the day and it was incongruous to hear the rattle of spent bullets falling on the tin roof of a hut in which one was being lectured on Military Law or how to come to the aid of the civil power, a procedure predicated on colonial service.

Then one day the whole remote, archaic pattern was broken. It was a fine summer morning and the hut was uncomfortably hot. I was resting my head on my hand, pretending to be industriously taking notes but in fact nodding off from time to time. The subject, on this occasion, almost unbelievably, was Official Correspondence and a regular officer was demonstrating on a blackboard the correct forms of the DO (or demi-official) letter and the acceptance of an invitation to dinner from the Governor (they never taught us how to decline) when the order came for us to report to our company parade ground. Within an hour we were in trucks on our way to Frinton-on-Sea, some twenty miles away across the flat marshlands of Essex.

Frinton is a sedate resort, much favoured by English parents for that month by the sea to which the children and Nanny are dispatched, and if Mother goes too it does not

71

count as her holiday, which takes place later with Father, to Scotland or perhaps abroad. That at least was the pattern of twenty years ago. But Frinton in the summer of 1940 was deserted, the villas stood empty, and the only hotel open was, until our arrival, frequented only by coastal gunners and some naval officers whose function I never knew.

My company was installed in a handsome villa called Maryland, the name reputedly having an association with the Duchess of Windsor, who comes from Baltimore. So handsome, indeed, was the villa that we were at once ordered to remove our boots in the porch and walk about the parquet floors and the bare stairs only in stockinged feet, to hammer no nails in the walls (a favourite habit of soldiers), and to ensure that no kitbags or equipment touched the walls, which were painted in pastel colours. This last requirement was difficult for me, as I had been detailed to take charge of a section—seven men—and allocated a bedroom (pale pink and, of course, unfurnished) which I think the civilian owner would have offered to a solo house guest only with an apology for cramping him. By the time eight of us were disposed about the floor, leaving a *cordon sanitaire* round the walls, it meant that there was a tangle of legs and kit everywhere. However the sleeping problem was not too serious, as during our tenancy sleep consisted mainly of what we could achieve during two hours compulsory rest every afternoon from 2.30 to 4.30.

As the weather was fine, our meals were served out of doors, and the arrangements were so haphazard that it was easy enough to slip away at 1 o'clock to the hotel, so long as we were back by 2.30 and huddled on the bedroom floor to satisfy the Sergeant who came round to check. We slipped away because the food was indescribably bad—I think all the proper cooks had been left behind at the barracks—and also because drink was our only solace during this uncomfortable period. The result was that for ten days or so I lived on lager (spirits were unobtainable) and cold sausage rolls. Thus my two hours' rest was largely spent crunching anti-dyspepsia tablets and I was very short of sleep indeed. (I found, by the way, that after a few days one achieved a sort of subnormality which became one's norm; permanently tired but able to function, permanently dyspeptic but almost unable to remember having been anything else.)

The object of our excursion was to hold a stretch of coast against possible invasion until we were relieved by evacuated troops from France after they had been re-formed and re-fitted. But we were cadets, and all our officers and NCOs were instructors, and they were dutiful men with a training programme to carry out. So by day they took us out on tactical exercises of various kinds and by night we guarded our given strategic points.

I was allocated with my section to guard the pier at the adjacent resort of Walton-on-the-Naze. In this duty, I was told, we would alternate with another section, whose equally temporary commander was a fine, tough fellow-Scot named Douglas. For an illusory moment I wondered if this meant that on the other nights we would be off duty. But all it meant was that my section would then be responsible for a different guard. This was a children's school, where some of our company and most of the equipment and ammunition were housed. This guard at least provided occasional periods of comparative rest, for half the section was enough to picket the place.

We made our headquarters in the cloakroom of the school, which afforded us some simple amusement at first, as everything was on a miniature scale; the coat pegs were about three feet off the ground, the basins were tiny and much lower, and the lavatory seats were not more than eighteen inches high. It was like living in a biggish doll's house.

The floor was tiled and unaccommodating, so between

73

guards the men sat around uncomfortably in full kit, or lay down if they could find a tolerable way to do so. I was responsible for checking in the men living in the building, so I found a place for myself just inside the door, but unfortunately under one of those miniature wash basins. I soon found that I sat up abruptly so often and hit my already woozy head on the basin that I took to lying down with my steel helmet on, which anybody who has tried it will know is a feat in itself. But so desperate were we for any form of rest that I did it, and I can still hear the crash of steel on porcelain as I arose to change a guard or make a tour of inspection.

The Walton pier guard was, at least in theory, much more dramatic. It was a long pier and at the far end, alone with seven men on a dark night, one could not but be conscious that only the misty North Sea lay between us and German-occupied Holland, from which who knows what adventurous invaders might arrive at any moment.

My section and I were delivered there at dusk on the first evening. We trudged out the length of the pier and found that it ended in a blank wall of sandbags from which one had been removed to form a spyhole for a sentry. There was a small theatre at the pier-end, with the bills of the last show still readable though stained and tattered. A door was open (or did we break it open?) and we made our guardroom in a dressing room with access to a lavatory. It was, by any standards, an odd situation and as each soldier's rifle and ten rounds of ammunition were our total defensive power it was hard to see us as an invasion-repelling force.

We had seen nobody since we arrived and looking at the length of the pier I made gloomy calculations as to how long a runner would take to report to any effective force headquarters—even if I knew where one was to be found. It was at this point, I'm afraid, that I remarked that we were clearly intended to make Britain a land fit for pierrots to live in,

74

which evoked no reaction whatever from my companions. If they heard, they were too sunk in gloom for feeble jokes or too young to understand.

The sentry's spyhole worried me. In relation to its field of vision—roughly speaking, the North Sea—it was far too small, rather like looking through a pinhole in a sheet of paper and causing the same effect of eye-fatigue through concentration. With the mist swirling about at sea the effect after a few minutes was almost irresistibly soporific. I toyed with the idea of detailing a second sentry to keep the peephole man awake, but decided I had better take responsibility for this myself as—with submarines, rubber boats, and frogmen in mind—I felt our entire strength should be engaged in patrolling the pier.

Our first and only contact with the outside world came with the arrival of a Royal Artillery major apparently responsible for the coastal defences in this area. He was very brusque and military, and obviously had little time to spare.

'Everything under control? Your men all right?'

He was about to turn on his heel when I put my question about how I should report anything that happened. The major frowned impatiently.

'Telephone us at HQ,' he said, 'I'll give you the number.'

I wrote it down.

'But where do I telephone *from?*' I asked.

He pointed with his swagger stick into the landward murk.

'There's a call box at the end of the pier,' he said.

Even by this time, and with all my anxiety not to make a wrong step as a cadet, I could not restrain myself.

'You mean,' I said, and the tone was no more correct than the words, 'that if the enemy arrive I can let you know provided I've got two pennies in my pocket.'

But he was sarcasm-proof.

'Have you?' he asked.

75

I fished out my money.

'Yes.'

'Good show,' he said, and stamped off.

My dislike of this officer was unimportant and irrational. My next night on the pier guard he turned up about 2 a.m., was rightly offered every possible obstacle by the first of my patrol who encountered him, and was eventually led to me with a rifle in his back. I was delighted.

'Turn out the guard,' he barked.

I echoed the bark and my section formed up with commendable speed considering the dark and the distance over which they were scattered. He walked down the tiny line peering at them.

'Six men,' he said. 'You're supposed to have seven. Seven men and yourself.'

I realised what had happened, but I was in no mood to be put in the wrong by this character.

'No, sir,' I said firmly. 'Six men. Definitely six men and myself.'

He grunted and vanished.

Over by the spyhole, in a pier deckchair we had rigged up on a wooden stand so that the sentry's eyes would be on a level with the aperture, my guard was sound asleep. With the optical conditions as they were, and as I had taken it upon myself to keep the sentry awake, I could not blame him.

Through those long-seeming nights nothing at all happened. We walked about the pier, stared at the sea, watched the sun come up, and were duly carted back to Maryland for breakfast and the day's training. Then one evening I saw my friend Douglas and his section off for their turn of pier guard. The Sergeant-Major inspected them and went indoors before they drove off. Not long afterwards I was getting my section ready to march off to our doll's house school when Douglas's truck drove up and the men started

76

to clamber down. The Sergeant-Major appeared in the porch and scowled.

'What the hell . . .' he exploded. 'Why haven't you . . . get off to that bloody pier and don't hang about . . .'

Douglas looked up from his unloading and gave an impudent grin. 'There *is* no bloody pier,' he said.

That day we had heard some explosions, but didn't know what they were. Higher authority had decided that it was better to put the pier out of action than to guard it, so the Sappers had blown up the middle of it, but such was the co-ordination of information at the time that nobody had bothered to tell us.

Next day we were relieved by a company of a Scottish infantry regiment. There was no formal hand-over. We piled out as they piled in. Nobody had given them any orders about being kind to the parquet and as I left I watched them clumping about in their nailed boots. When I looked around our little pink bedroom, to make sure nothing had been left behind, men were hammering nails into the walls and hanging up their equipment.

Back at our barracks at Colchester we all went straight to bed although it was early evening. I had been conscious of a nagging pain in my back for the last day or two, but thought I was lucky to get away with no more than stiffness after all the hard lying of Frinton. But next morning I knew it for what it was—lumbago. I reported sick to the Sergeant-Major who looked at me oddly. 'Pains in the back, eh,' he said. 'You're quite an old soldier already, aren't you?'

This mystified me and I sought an explanation from somebody more experienced. He told me that the most notorious malingerer's complaints were pains in the back or pains in the head—hard to identify, harder to check, and always good for a spell of light duties, or better.

I was still under MO's orders a couple of days later when my comrades were summoned out on night road blocks,

77

another favourite diversion of the period. I was alone in the barrack block and had occasion to go past the company commander's office. The door was unlocked. I had heard of our report cards, which some of the cadets had seen, with exciting annotations like 'Will make a good officer' or 'Natural leader'. Stealthily I shone my torch on the desk. There was a card index. I riffled nervously through to the Ws and found my card. It recorded my Army history briefly and without comment. I turned the card over. On the back it said 'Platoon Commander's Comments'. Against 'First Month' he had written 'Average' and against 'Second Month' and 'Third Month' he had merely added ditto marks. It was the most terse and accurate verdict on my Army career I was ever to see.

6

THE RED BOBBLE

The first time I wore the uniform of an officer in the British Army I went to lunch with friends in the country. It was a Sunday in the late summer of 1940 and I was due to report to my regiment the following day. The uniform had been delivered the previous day and I was desperately trying to break it in. Not only did it look distressingly new and unlived-in but after nearly a year in the ranks I felt self-consciously grand in fine barathea, collar and tie, and shining leather Sam Browne belt.

There were about a dozen guests and I knew only half of them. We were having drinks on the lawn when a dowager-ish lady I didn't know walked up to me, ran what seemed to me a rather cold eye over me and said, 'Ah, the 60th Rifles—salt of the earth, eh? Don't dine,' and before I could think of anything to say she had drifted away.

It was only after I had been with the regiment for some time that I solved this mystery by telling a senior officer the story. All I learned at the time was that the lady was the widow of a colonel of The Buffs. The explanation of her dislike of my regiment—it seemed unfair on me as I hadn't yet joined—was that her husband's battalion and a battalion of the 60th—the King's Royal Rifle Corps—had once, before the war, been brigaded together in Burma. The man who elucidated for me was a regular soldier and he laughed when I told him the story. The 'salt of the earth' part was simply that she believed the 60th to be overloaded with regimental pride, which may be true but is certainly not unique; the 'don't dine' addendum arose from the fact that the 60th, having their own Mess customs, were not much given to dining out in Messes which they found less agreeable than their own.

I had been surprised myself, on arrival at my battalion, which was encamped on a heath in Wiltshire, to find that the Mess was very different from those of which I had had a worm's eye glimpse while in the ranks. Only the Commanding Officer was addressed as 'Sir'; even the fierce, Prussian-headed adjutant, to whom I found it difficult to speak without standing to attention, was addressed as 'Dinky' after working hours.

There were no set places either in the ante-room (I have seen Messes with three immovable armchairs round the fire —reserved for the CO, the second-in-command, and the adjutant) or in the dining room. You sat where you pleased and if you were late for dinner you apologised to the first person you encountered on entering. This was liable to have an alarming consequence for the timid, newly-joined subaltern, who almost certainly took the first seat inside the door. Many times I watched the expression on the face of such a young man when, on his first night, he found an arm round his shoulder, heard an amiable voice saying, 'I'm frightfully sorry, old boy,' and looked up into the face of his Commanding Officer.

This Colonel was one of the gentlest, kindest, most attractive human beings I have ever known—qualities which in no way interfered with his capability, his sternness when necessary, and his implacable insistence on what is known as 'care of men'. If a dusk patrol was due back in camp at, say, eight o'clock, and the subaltern in charge of it appeared in Mess, spruced up, at 8.10, I would note the Colonel's mild eye turned on him and pity the subaltern for what was coming to him next morning. For obviously he could not have checked in his patrol, disposed of the vehicles and weapons, and seen his men settled down to their special late supper. He was guilty on the 'care of men' count and he would suffer for it.

On the other hand, it was the same Colonel who said something I never forgot: 'Any bloody fool can be uncomfortable.' This dictum was uttered one bitterly cold dawn when we were out on an exercise and I happened to be with the CO when he discovered that an over-zealous platoon commander had made his men sleep in a ditch when there was a nearby barn available.

The Colonel was as full of regimental pride as anybody. Once at a Mess meeting a brash subaltern rose and asked why, as the Army provided one-and-sixpence a day for an officer's messing, and most regiments charged only one-and-sixpence more for 'luxuries', we paid four-and-six a day extra. What was the three shillings for? The Mess president, a bumbling, dugout major, looked flustered, but the Colonel fixed the young man with his eye and said quietly, 'For the red bobble on your hat'. There was, you will see, a good deal of snobbery in the 60th and there was no future in kicking against it.

We fared excellently. There was an Army School of Cookery in the same camp, all the officer-instructors of which were chefs or restaurateurs. When an 'austerity' order was issued that all Messes must have one cold supper night a week some of my fellow officers simply went out with their guns in off-duty hours and turned in the bag to the caterers. The result was that our cold supper table looked like a colour-ad in the shiny magazines, featuring such items as grouse, pâté de compagne and hare-in-burgundy pie, *garni* with vegetables grown around the doors.

There was clothes snobbery too. Every new officer's joining instructions included the names of the tailor, hatter, shirtmaker, and leather shop he should go to—all with

81

London, S.W.1, addresses. My favourite line in the instructions read: 'There is hunting, shooting and golf, so bring what plain clothes you want.' 'Plain clothes' itself was a snobbery; the common Army word 'mufti' was not used. Similarly, whereas most regiments call their undress button-up-to-the-throat evening wear 'blues' or 'patrols' ours were 'black serge'. It was not allowed, for good reason at that time, to enforce the wearing of patrols (an officer's kit allowance did not rise to the expense anyhow), but they were generally worn in the 60th. To satisfy authority, however, the Standing Orders of the Mess permitted an officer to dine in service dress with a black silk shirt and black tie. Nobody ever did so—or rather one young man did, once. He was a swarthy, aquiline young man and he suddenly found the Adjutant asking him if a certain hut would suit his purpose, what furniture he would require, and when he wanted his men paraded in the morning. It was some time before the misunderstanding was sorted out. The combination of our black buttons and the black tie had convinced the Adjutant that this must be the touring Jewish chaplain whose visit was imminent.

But the snobberies were not personal; new officers were accepted or not on their merits. I think I was the only non-Public School subaltern of my period with the battalion, and I was certainly the only ex-Sapper; the general attitude was that county regiments were uncouth and such corps as the Royal Engineers, freaks one rarely encountered; but the only reaction I ever had was a look of shocked surprise when I mentioned where I had served in the ranks. On the other hand when an intolerably affected and arrogant young man turned up, with a noble name and every paper qualification, and was posted to the company of which I was temporarily in command, the Colonel simply sent for me and with the Adjutant present said, 'I imagine you could do without So-and-so.' I agreed that I could. The Colonel looked at the

Adjutant and murmured, 'Somebody must want an ADC somewhere . . .' and within a day or two the man was gone.

The average age of the subalterns was considerably below my twenty-nine. Most of my life had been spent among people older than myself and it was a shock to find that I was relatively senior in years. But it had its advantages. When my elderly Company Commander (he had come back to help out and now held the same rank as he had in 1918) found I was what he regarded as a 'responsible age' and had some organisational ability he unofficially appointed me his deputy and delegated so thoroughly that while it was flattering it was also harassing. He would take the early parade and then go off ratting with his dogs, leaving the rest to me. On cold days he would turn up later in the morning and march me off to the Mess for cherry brandy 'elevenses'.

All the 'employed' men of the battalion, as distinct from soldiers in training, were on the strength of our company, so I was responsible for a strange assortment of barbers, soldier-servants ('batmen' was a non-60th word), store-keepers, cooks, drivers, medical orderlies, lavatory orderlies, and even poultry and gardening orderlies—the camp was a permanent one and well equipped for self-supply.

The trouble with employed men is that they are apt to get lost—and not accidentally. There is nothing a cook or a batman resents more than a parade. For census purposes more than anything else, we had a weekly parade of these otherwise autonomous characters. One day a subaltern sent a note to say his servant would not be on parade as he had been sent shopping to the nearest town. I intercepted the note and the man was not missed by the Company Com-mander. In Mess I sought out the subaltern and in what I hoped was a comradely way suggested that, from my know-ledge of the Company Commander's temperament, it would have been awkward if he had received the note. He was grateful and later told a friend of mine that he had been

83

given a very useful tip by—he had forgotten the name, but that subaltern who's getting on a bit. It was about this time I realised that, with a forage cap on, all my visible hair was grey, moving steadily to white.

It was a curiously varied performance I had to give, playing paternal old-soldier to new officers and trying to conceal from old soldiers how new an officer I was. Every morning a little procession of minor offenders was brought before me at Company Office and to get through this task as quickly as possible I evolved a simple formula. Having heard the charge and what the man had to say, I would decide that no more than an unrecorded reprimand was necessary, so the dialogue usually went something like this:

'How long have you been in the Army?'

'Three months, sir.'

'Well, it's long enough for you to know that . . .'

I must have become a little glib with this for one day a soldier answered my first question with 'Ten years, sir', and I had gone on some way with my routine homily before I realised what he had said, did a double-take, and had to back-pedal in a floundering way which must have been good for a laugh at my expense in the NAAFI.

After the offenders, there were sometimes the soldiers who wished to exercise their right to an interview with their officer. Usually it was a personal matter, like compassionate leave. One morning a rifleman was marched in and when asked what he wanted to say rapped out, 'Sir, I've broken my *piyala*. Sir.'

The Sergeant-Major was at my elbow and there was the inevitable small audience of NCOs and office staff. I wished I had assumed it was a personal matter and sent them out. As it was I couldn't appeal to them without losing face.

'Well,' I said, 'how did you do that?'

'Coming out of the dining hall, sir. Slipped and fell, sir.'

84

I looked him over. He seemed to be all in one unmaimed piece.

'So what do you propose to do about it?'

'Report to you, sir. Then to the Quartermaster.'

'Good,' I said. 'Dismiss.'

When they had all gone but the Sergeant-Major I asked for a translation. The Sergeant-Major was astonished I didn't know that a *piyala* was a cup or mug and that the soldier was following the correct procedure in reporting the breakage before drawing a new one and having the cost deducted from his pay. The Sergeant-Major assumed that everybody knew those Hindi words with which soldiers who have served in India pepper their conversation. He didn't know that I had only recently learned that *dhobie* meant laundry.

The system by which a soldier can apply for an interview with his officer, up to the Colonel, without disclosing reasons, is an admirable one and often solves human problems in a humane way. A good example was when a soldier asked to see me and, tense with urgency, asked to be put on a draft which was being formed for overseas. I explained to him that these drafts were made up on the basis of reports from NCOs and platoon officers and the consensus was that he was not yet sufficiently trained to qualify.

I thought he was simply a soldier who was keen to get on active service. Almost immediately another rifleman sought an interview and asked to be taken *off* the same draft. He was a pleasant, intelligent young man and he too was intensely anxious to achieve what he wanted. I couldn't understand it. I toyed for a moment with the idea of exchanging these two men, but decided I must abide by the reports on proficiency. So I denied his request too.

But when I dismissed him he stood still, blushing and looking over my head. I waited, and with the utmost difficulty he said he did not want to be parted from Rifleman

85

A—which at least explained the two consecutive appeals. I immediately scented homosexuality, which sounds drastic but is inevitable. I simply asked why they were so anxious to stay together. Again there was a long pause. 'We're mates,' he said at last; that was all, yet I felt there was something more to it.

I sent for the sergeant of the platoon both men were in and asked him to try to find out discreetly what lay behind this. It did not take him long. Rifleman A had a secret; he was illiterate, or very nearly so. Rifleman B was teaching him to read and write in private. It had cost A a great effort to confess his secret to his mate and he could not face confiding in somebody else; they wanted to complete the tuition. I took B off the draft and eventually sent them on another one together.

A disproportionate amount of my time seemed to be taken up with delinquency, military or civil. Apart from the daily 'crime sheet' there were occasional courts martial, appearances in the police courts of neighbouring towns as 'prisoner's friend', and even, on one occasion, which I shall describe in another connection, a journey to London to give 'evidence of character' in a case against a rifleman.

The first time I appeared at a court martial I took infinite pains with my case for the defence. I interviewed the prisoner—a deserter—in the guardroom several times, sorted out the obvious lies from the more plausible parts of his story and, discovering that the essence of desertion lies in the intention not to return, built up an elaborate argument to show that the man had intended to come back, or at least that he could not be proved to have intended otherwise. This last became difficult when it emerged belatedly, via the civilian police, that he had flogged—that is, sold— every stitch of his military clothing and every piece of his equipment.

My case got off to a bad start. The President of the Court

86

asked me if I was making a plea in mitigation and seemed rather impatient when I said no, I had a complete defence to offer. The Court fidgeted and seemed bored; the Judge Advocate looked, to me at least, half amused and half contemptuous. A sense of injustice spurred me on, and there is no doubt that it spurred me too far and too long.

The sentence was 112 days' detention. Leaving the court I met an officer of another company who had been very helpful to me; he had once been the commandant of a military prison. He put his hand on my shoulder and said something to the effect that that was quite a speech I had made. It was nice of him to say so, I replied unhappily, but it hadn't had much effect, had it? Oh, yes, he said. A considerable effect.

'How?' I asked, irritably.

'Well,' he said thoughtfully, 'I've seen a lot of those cases, you know, and I would say that without your speech he would probably have got fifty-six days.'

If I defended that prisoner too much there was one I defended too little, indeed not at all. He was a camp hospital orderly, summoned to a police court about six miles away. I was particularly busy on the morning of the case and sent a message to the hospital that the rifleman should report to the Company Office and I would drive him into town. My idea was that he could tell me the facts on the way. But a message came back that the rifleman had already left. I realised I had cut everything rather fine and left at once. But by the time I reached the court my man was already in the dock and there was no chance of consulting him. I was in time to hear the charge, which was that he had taken a motor bicycle without the owner's permission and ridden it without a licence; also that he had stolen a blanket and a groundsheet. He pleaded not guilty.

The Chief Constable took him through the story to the point where it was established that he had, in fact, taken the

87

articles. Why? asked the Chief Constable. And why did he plead not guilty?

The rifleman was a regular soldier with a row of service chevrons. He stood like a ramrod in the dock, head slightly raised, looking ahead and upward over the Bench, and he spoke as if delivering a well-rehearsed recitation.

'Well, sir,' he said, 'it was like this, sir. There was a dance at the camp that night, sir. I wanted to take a girl home, sir.'

The Chief Constable asked patiently what that had to do with the charge. Why had he taken the articles in question?

'Well, sir. It was like this, sir. There was a dance at the camp that night, sir. I wanted to take a girl home, sir.'

All right, said the Chief Constable. He wanted to take the girl home; that was why he took the bicycle, believing the owner would have lent it if asked. But why did he take a blanket and a groundsheet?

'Well, sir. It was like this, sir . . .'

The whole routine came out again, not an inflection varied. The Chief Constable interrupted.

'Why,' he asked wearily, 'did you take a blanket and a groundsheet?'

Suddenly the soldier relaxed his rigid posture, looked down at the Chief Constable, and in a totally different voice, full of challenging contempt for his interrogator's obtuseness, he said, 'Y'wouldn't like me to tell you, wouldya?'

All I did in that case was pay the five-pound fine which was quickly imposed and arrange for it to be deducted from his pay.

When I wasn't being an ineffective lay lawyer I was often an employment agent. The company's roll included a number of men who were drawing specialist rates of pay but for whom we had no job in their specialised line. When a specialist was wanted anywhere the application came to me. One day the Adjutant telephoned that a cook was required urgently at a Stately Home some miles away which had been requisitioned as a high level military headquarters. I consulted the Sergeant-Major; we went over our list of cooks and chose one. He was sent for and seemed a very presentable man. I gave instructions for him to be driven, with his kit, to his new and cosy-sounding job.

That evening, passing a bunch of soldiers in a camp roadway, I thought I saw the cook, then decided I must be mistaken. But the thought persisted and I sent for the Sergeant-Major. Oh, no, he said, I must be mistaken. He had personally seen the cook off in a truck with all his kit. I told him to enquire. Half an hour later he reported back. I was right. Our cook was home again. The Sergeant-Major asked him what had happened. 'I don't know,' the man said, looking genuinely puzzled. 'I'd only just got there and I was in the kitchen and a sergeant came down and said the General wanted tea. He had company up in the drawing room. Wanted it right away. Well, when I took the pail up . . .'

Nobody had ticked him off. He had simply and immediately been ordered back to where he came from. He probably established a record for short tenure as a General's cook, but I should like to have been present at the moment in the drawing room when tea was served.

It was ironic that while I was trying to deal with the problems of the 'employed' men I had also to cope with a less constant but trying problem of unemployed men. The main body of the company was fully engaged in a training programme but there were at times quite large numbers of men who had completed their training and were waiting to be drafted overseas.

No soldier is more difficult to handle than the idle soldier, and none is quicker to realise when duties or training are designed more to prevent boredom or to keep him out of mischief than to further his proficiency. The draftee is

89

restless, impatient, and apt to see no reason why he shouldn't be on embarkation leave until it is time for him to go abroad. When, as sometimes happened, a man had had embarkation leave twice and was still hanging about a camp in England, his morale was unpredictable, even from day to day.

One sternly devised further training programmes and tried to stress their importance, but the scepticism was palpable. It was better to be unorthodox—so long as higher authority didn't find out—and intersperse their days with what were frankly games. When influenza struck down several platoon commanders I was reduced to putting bodies of these men under one NCO and offering a packet of cigarettes to the first man to reach the top of a nearby hill— stressing, of course, the need for maintaining a high pitch of physical fitness—or sending them out in pairs on 'initiative tests', which amused them, gave them some freedom, and at least got them out from under my feet.

All the trained men had qualified in D and M (driving and maintenance) and when I was given two buses for use in the company's defensive rôle in the event of invasion I packed off whole groups to practise bus driving. I discovered that men who had driven even heavy vehicles for years took some time to get the knack of handling a bus and, though their military careers were unlikely to call for such a skill, this again kept them busy on something a little off the beaten track of routine.

Nearly all the men were Londoners, and home was only a couple of hours hitch-hiking away; so absenteeism became rife. It was coolly calculated. They knew that if they had a few days at home and were put in the guardroom when they returned they would be released if the draft movement order came through, so what had they to lose?

When Christmas came we had a mass of unauthorised departures. A pale-faced corporal reported one night that his entire barrack room was deserted. He had found a packet of cigarettes on his pillow with a message attached—'Happy Christmas, Corp'—and signed by all the missing men. The temptation to take no action, knowing they would all be back as soon as the holiday was over, was great, but one could not take that easy way. I had the local police of each man's home district informed and a sufficient number of them spent their Christmas in civilian cells to serve as a warning to others.

The various invasion alarms were almost a relief in that they called for action which at least approximated to war, though nothing in fact happened. The company's task was to guard the perimeter of an airfield a few miles away. When the alarm stand-by was received our curious caravan set off—two buses, a couple of jeeps, and two dispatch riders.

We were assigned our rôle only when the first of these alarms was received, so we arrived at the airfield in the dark. Two World War I soldiers, now ground defence officers in the RAF, greeted us. My first question was as to the extent of the perimeter. It was nine miles. My training told me that you should never spread men thinly, so I split my force into two small mobile units (each with a bus) and proposed to hold them in a central position while pickets covered the perimeter. But the RAF men would have none of this and it was made clear to me that once on their premises I came under their orders. So I had the ridiculous task of spreading my men—about 120 of them—along a nine-mile line. The RAF men supervised my placing of them and apparently approved. When dawn came I found that most of them had a field of fire which could have caused them only to shoot up the anti-aircraft gunners on the rising ground around us.

We were out for two days and nights and most of my time was spent trying to organise the feeding of the men, which could only be done by the two buses and the jeeps almost permanently touring and the men getting their meals at

91

extraordinary times. Fortunately I found some vacuum containers in the airfield headquarters and took them without asking, so that some of the food reached the men hot.

When the alarm was over and we returned to camp on a Saturday I found that I was due to take part as an instructor in a Home Guard night exercise. I was also due for forty-eight hours' leave. The Adjutant was apologetic about this muddle, but the best that could be worked out was that I could go on leave the moment the exercise was over, which was dawn on Sunday.

Before dark on the Saturday night I went out to look over the arrangements for the part of the exercise for which I was responsible. I had put on service dress instead of battle dress, in order to be ready to get away promptly, and hoped that with my greatcoat on nobody would notice. I also wore a new pair of shoes which I had had made in London as a luxurious gesture against the long months I had spent in heavy service boots. Prices had gone up and my shoemaker charged something like fourteen guineas, which I regarded (and still do regard) as far too much to spend on a pair of shoes. Approaching one concealed emplacement on my rounds I said, 'What you need here is a trip wire', and at that second fell flat on my face; not only was the trip wire there but it was beautifully concealed. The toe-cap of one of my new shoes was ripped across by the barbed wire. I had mentioned my extravagance to one or two of my friends and from then these shoes were known as Watts's Folly.

In the morning I stopped only to shave and then drove into the nearest town to catch the London train. I found a first-class compartment with three corners occupied. I knew all three travellers by sight—indeed two of them I had met casually. They were an actress, an actor, and a producer, on their way back from a show in the West Country. They proceeded to discuss theatrical affairs and personalities with no discretion whatever. When they talked about friends of mine I became almost embarrassed as well as amused. But I knew that uniform is a wonderful bestower of anonymity. Nobody in khaki could possibly know the people they were talking about, usually by Christian names. They gossiped, they tore at reputations, and slandered outrageously. I felt a world away from the Army and was fascinated; I wish I had been able to stay awake.

7

TABLE FOR EIGHT

ONE CONSEQUENCE of a peace that lasts as long as twenty-one years is that a generation grows up with a lot of false ideas about war. Depending on which country they lived in before 1939, the members of a peace-raised generation matured in the belief that war was (*a*) their duty and their destiny, besides being a lot of fun, or (*b*) an improbable nightmare which, because of laboratory and workshop developments, would end civilisation as they knew it in twenty-four hours. The mental picture conditioning the outlook was either a Nuremberg rally or a Korda–Wells set from 'Things to Come'. Then, when war started again and as it went on, these preconceived ideas and theories were battered aside by experience.

Take this, for example: many young men in Britain, myself certainly among them, used to say, 'They'll never bomb London. Of course, if they did, it would be knocked flat in a couple of hours. But by then our planes would be doing the same to Berlin. So you see, it cancels out. They might as well stay at home and bomb themselves out of existence.' This piece of *reductio ad absurdum* comforted us mightily.

Then, when we used to talk about personal danger from bombing, we always said, after learnedly discussing the effects of blast and flying masonry, 'But, of course, if you get a direct hit—well, it's just too bad.' We didn't linger on that. We knew. We knew a man who had been in the Spanish civil war. I had it most certainly fixed at the back of my head that you couldn't be in a building when it took a direct hit and live. Some eighteen months later, in the spring of 1941,

94

I had at the back of my head a neat surgical dressing about an inch square which proved me wrong. I had been in a building when it took a direct hit—two direct hits, the official communiqué said—and I was alive to tell this tale.

London was always my leave goal. Leave and London—they teamed up in my mind like Crosse and Blackwell or Lunt and Fontanne. Then, for the first time, Army business took me to London. London *between* leaves—it was almost too good to be true. The British Army, fatherly even to the miscreant, always sends an officer to a police court where a soldier is appearing as a defendant to do what he can on the prisoner's behalf, and I was ordered to London one Saturday to represent a man in such a case. The proceedings were short and I was free before lunch; the rest of the week-end was mine. I telephoned friends all over town. My luck was good, and by seven that evening our party in the Ritz bar had swollen to seventeen. One of the men happened to be passing through from one war station to another, a second had wangled a night's leave from the country, and so on. There were a number of girls, too. Several of us had not seen each other since the dear, dead days before the war, when a night out in the West End was a thing of pleasant routine rather than an exciting novelty.

Some had other engagements and wandered off. Finally, we got down to eight, all set to make an evening of it. Where should we go? The familiar haunts were reviewed, and we took expert advice from those who had been staying in London. There was an Alert on. Which spots were best for escaping blackout and blitz? The Café de Paris, having already survived one bomb, beat the Savoy by a narrow margin, and after them came the Suivi, the brightest of the current night clubs. We telephoned, booked tables, and organised ourselves.

The sky was bright with flares when we came out into Piccadilly. A man in my taxi wanted to call at his club in

95

Pall Mall. While he was inside, I stood on the pavement looking at the flares, which were coming down thicker than ever. Then I heard my first bomb whistle. Everybody had told me how a whistling bomb always seemed to be coming straight for one's own head, and I now confirmed the truth of this. The high-pitched 'whee-ee-ee' went on at least twice as long as it seemed reasonable for any missile to take to drop. The instinct to hunch the shoulders and sink the head was irresistible. When at last the 'crrump' came, it sounded surprisingly far away. Back in the taxi I made a foolish remark. 'Thank heaven we're going to the Café,' I said. 'No place is ever hit twice.'

As we got out of the taxi at the door of the Café another whistler came down—louder and nearer. A few people on the crowded pavement dived into shop doorways. One frightened woman took a header down the Café steps, butting from behind and toppling over a girl in evening dress, who, at the end of *her* fall, sat up and ruefully examined a tear in one of her precious silk stockings. Quite possibly her last pair, I thought.

I had often been told by experienced Londoners that the best antidote for raid nerves was to go into a busy, gay place where a good band was playing and where what was happening outside was quickly forgotten. It worked well that night. Waiting in the lobby while the girls were leaving their wraps we discussed the little flurry we had seen outside. By the time we reached our table on the balcony I had forgotten there was a raid on.

'Stephen is the country cousin now,' somebody said, referring to the fact that after having long been a West End parishioner I had become, as a soldier, an out-of-towner. 'Give him the ring-side seat so that he can see all the smart people.' I was elaborately ushered into a chair next to the balcony rail, and we ordered our first course. I took one of the girls downstairs to dance. We danced a couple of numbers. 'Isn't this *fun!*' she said, as thrilled as a debutante. War certainly brushes up the simpler enthusiasms. 'Like old times,' I said. 'But for the uniforms, you'd never know there was a war on.' I seemed to have a gift that night for ominous fatuity.

When the band started to play 'Oh Johnny' we danced around to the stairs and went back up to our table. I was just tackling my smoked salmon when the girl on my right said to me, 'You know about such things. How much would you say Duggy Byng gets in cabaret here? We've been arguing.' A man on the other side of the table said, 'My guess is about twenty-five pounds a week.' I leaned forward to explain the facts of cabaret life to the innocent. 'I've known acts here to get five hundred pounds a week,' I started to say. 'Bunch Keys, I know, turned down as much as that once——' But I'll never be sure just how much of that sentence I uttered and how much was rammed back down my throat in a thick composition of dust and powdered mortar.

This is where the story is apt to become dull and difficult. Dull because in plain words all that happened was a big bang and the lights went out. Difficult because a statement like that doesn't begin to give any impression, to convey anything of the feeling of what happened.

It was all one compact happening. (If the official communiqué says there were two bombs, all right, there were two bombs, but there was only one bang.) One second everything was normal—music, bright lights, conversation, the luxurious litter of a crowded dinner table before me, a smart, substantial restaurant around me. Next second—palpable, pitch darkness, thick with noxious fumes (a smell I shall never forget) and dust you pulled down chokingly into your lungs with every breath. You sensed the chaos and wreckage all round and that colossal bang still reverberated in spine and stomach and head.

97

It is easy to use the glib, old-fashioned, true-blue British phrases like 'There was no panic' and 'People were magnificent.' It is harder to make those simple truths convincing. There was a moment of scattered, small noises, of people calling—they did not scream—to others in their now invisible parties. (I know if we had been separated, if any of my party had been dancing at the time, I should have called out to them.) But after that moment there was complete silence. Then the faraway voice of one of my friends said, 'Keep away from the edge of the balcony,' and I moved slowly and carefully around to the other side of the table.

My chin hurt. It had hit the table, I realised, when the bang came. We felt for one another, patting shoulders and gripping hands, and gradually reassuring ourselves that we were all alive. I tried to say to the girl beside me 'Are you all right?' but no sound came. My mouth was like an overfilled ashcan. I spat dryly into the dark. I tried to clear my throat. At last a thin echo of a voice came out.

For the student of nervous reaction, I can set down a few personal observations of those moments. Except for my chin, I had no sensation of having been hit by anything. I was definitely not afraid or jittery. My senses were clear and alert and my mind seemed neither accelerated nor stunned. I remember most clearly of all a feeling of deep depression. I remember thinking, as my lungs and nostrils rebelled against the fumes and filth, 'The entrance must be blocked. We are probably trapped.' Also, 'Is there anything else to fall?' I remember, too, waiting with ears strained to catch the first crack or rumble of a collapse that might yet be to come. It did not come. For a moment I recalled the time I had been down a coal mine in my early teens, an experience I had not thought about for years; there had been the same pitch dark, evil-smelling fumes, and the same sense of being entombed. I thought of the girls whose hands I held but could not see, and wondered if we would all just stand here and die slowly.

98

They were both young and I was fond of them, and I felt sick with misery.

Here and there a cigarette-lighter flickered. Fire—that was a new thought, and I looked around in the dark. Probably a hundred or more cigarettes had been burning when the bomb fell. Waiters with spirit stoves must have been cooking at tables. There was the danger of escaping gas, too; those naked flames of lighters were surely foolish. But this was no time to stand still and debate potential dangers. Our hand-clasping chain had decided to move. Slowly, painfully slowly and blindly, we started in the direction of the door.

Then the blessed thing happened. From the darkness, somewhere toward the top of the stairs leading down to the dance floor, came a loud, calm voice. 'The entrance is clear,' it said, without haste. 'Come this way, slowly, and you'll all be outside in a few minutes.' Later the voice became personified in the bulky figure of an ARP warden wearing a steel helmet and a businessman's mackintosh. Coming in from the street, he must have sized up the situation in a second and made the one announcement every soul in that room wanted to hear. I knew that until somebody said to me 'The war is over,' no four words would ever be more welcome in my ears than the warden's 'The entrance is clear.'

Our chain moved forward. We made sure, with every step, that there was something to stand on. The balcony narrowed where it curved round to the stairs. Fully a hundred people beyond our table had to come the same way, yet during our journey to safety nobody attempted to pass or jostle us. It was more orderly and quiet than many a crowd leaving a theatre.

One of my friends, trying to balance himself as he stepped over a pile of debris, brushed his hand against my head and remarked that my hair was wet. 'Must be wine,' he said. That seemed reasonable enough to me and I thought no more of it. A moment later, during one of our halts, the

99

same man murmured to his wife: 'I told you we should have gone to the Savoy, darling.'

Near the door the wreckage was so bad our party could not keep the chain formation, but it was no longer necessary, anyhow, for there was enough light coming down from the street to see dim shapes. The girl nearest me suddenly said: 'We can't go on. There's somebody lying there.' I stooped and could just make out a woman's head and shoulders. I touched one shoulder, trying to move her. She was rigid, pinned by a small mountain of debris. As my eyes focused better, I noticed the red, flowery pattern of her dress and realised that she had been sitting at the table next to ours. I stepped over her. There was nothing else to be done for the moment, but I hated doing it.

We reached the lobby and the short flight of stairs leading up to the street. We were safe. The girls could easily find their own way out now. I turned back towards where I had left the woman lying pinned. An ARP man grabbed me by the shoulder and stopped me. I protested, gabbling something about the woman. Quietly he assured me that she would be taken care of and would I please go out? I realised that I was doing just the sort of thing I would criticise other people for doing—trying to go back and help and getting in the way when the experts were at work.

In the lobby I met the second-in-command of my battalion. His face was black. 'All right?' I asked. 'Fine.' He grinned. 'Good God,' I said, 'You've lost all your teeth!' I put my hand up to his face and some of the black on his teeth came away on my fingers. We both laughed and I passed on. I later found out that he was lying when he said he was all right. He knew he had been hit in the back. He had to go to a hospital, where it was discovered that something had entered his back through one shoulder blade and come out near the other, leaving an ugly little tunnel. How it missed his spine, nobody knew.

Outside, it was cool and pleasant and moonlit. I had one of the girls of our party in my charge now. For the first time I thought something must be wrong with the back of my head. My collar felt damp. I touched my head and looked at my hand. It was covered with dirt and blood. I looked at my uniform. The shoulders were dark red and blood was dripping from my lanyard. An ARP man directed me to take the girl I was with across the street. She was limp, and I put my arm round her and tried to speak encouragingly, telling her we had only a little way to go. Halfway across the street our positions were suddenly reversed. The air had revived her, but to my surprise my knees went weak and for the rest of the way she supported me.

We entered a shelter in the basement of an office building. Someone sent me to wash up. In the midst of disaster and tragedy there was nothing to do but laugh at my reflection in the mirror over the basin. My face looked as if it had been crudely made up with burnt cork, and my clotted hair was standing spikily on end. I took off my collar and tie and threw them away. They looked as if they had been soaked in burgundy.

A little man in a steel helmet bathed my head. Some nurses arrived. One of them came over to the man who was assiduously dressing my skull. 'What's this?' she demanded. '*Quite* the wrong thing.' And almost triumphantly, matching a swift rip to the first word, she whisked off the bandage. That was the first time my head had really hurt. When she had fixed a dressing to her satisfaction, she demanded my handkerchief and tied it around my head. I lit a cigarette. The lighter flame, I noticed, was steady.

The little man in the steel helmet had turned his attention to other patients and I looked round in time to see him dabbing with wet cottonwool at the face of a man in a dinner jacket, who seemed to have been even more blackened than I. Some dirt came away but the basic black remained. The patient was one of the coloured players from the Café band.

I went back to the restaurant. Even in the crowd around the door I could see that I was only in the way. The next problem was to rendezvous with the rest of our party and check that we were all safe. I decided to go to the Mayfair Hotel, where we knew two or three of our friends were staying. There were no taxis, so I started to walk with one of the girls. She began to shiver and her teeth were chattering. I was shivering too. I remembered that a person suffering from shock often doesn't know it.

Outside the Piccadilly Hotel we saw a taxi about to start off. We yelled and ran across the street, babbled something to the people in the dark inside, and piled in. They were obviously taken aback at the invasion, but they were accommodating about it and told the driver to take us to the Mayfair, although it wasn't in the direction they were going. We talked all the way, yet neither of us ever saw the faces of our hosts. Everybody sat on top of everybody else.

I had forgotten about my rather startling appearance. I strode into the bright, busy lounge of the Mayfair and marched up to the desk. It must have been an alarming sight —a dirty, collarless, blood-stained officer, his dishevelled hair bound in a khaki handkerchief, gypsy fashion. I was told that we were the first to arrive. Gradually the others turned up and told their stories. One man had tried to go home for fresh clothes but found there was an unexploded bomb in his street; on the way back he had considerately called at the Suivi and cancelled our table. Before leaving the wrecked Café, a girl who had been bombed twice before and each time lost a fur coat had gone to the cloakroom, presented her ticket, and recovered her wrap. 'I couldn't afford to lose *three* fur coats,' she explained.

Samaritans flocked around us in the lounge. I decided to forget the first-aid bit I'd learned about not allowing head injury cases to take spirits and drank several welcome brandies. The girls were whisked off to baths, with offers of cosmetics, stockings, and beds for the night. One elderly woman who kept trying to help in one way after another eventually produced her trump card, an Army doctor who had been dining and dancing downstairs. His partner came with him. I was taken to a bedroom to be attended by him. His attractive girl friend cut my hair around the wound most efficiently. 'You should have been a nurse,' I said admiringly. 'I am,' she replied.

At last our party dispersed to bed, but, as we found when we met again next day, in no case to sleep much. Another alert sounded early in the morning. In my case, it was the excuse I had been waiting for to get out of bed. My pillow looked like a gravel road after a minor accident. I was restless and very hungry. By a quarter past seven I was out walking in the West End.

I went back to the shattered Café. By one of those freaks which were a commonplace of bombing, the men's cloakroom was unscathed. Although it seemed wrong to be concerned about such things when one was lucky enough just to be alive, I admit I was glad to find my coat, hat, respirator, even gloves and stick. That awful smell still hung about the place. In a corridor I met a waiter who had been there all night. His dress suit was in rags, and his blackened shirtfront flapped before him absurdly as he walked. His face was grimy and his eyes bloodshot from strain and sleeplessness. At the ladies' cloakroom I was lucky again. All the women's wraps had been piled on the floor to make a resting place for the wounded. I had heard one of the girls describe a wrap she had lost—an elbow-length cape, ermine-lined. I saw a corner of ermine half buried in the pile and pulled. Out came the cape.

Later, in the sunny quiet of a Sunday morning, I drove down to the country with a man who had been in our party.

We had arranged to join the rest of the previous night's group for lunch at the home of a friend in Hampshire. Without preface, as we motored along, my companion suddenly said, quietly and reflectively, 'It must have been a very small bomb.' It was a thought, I suppose, we had all had, yet none of us had felt like mentioning it. One is always tempted to think of one's own personal bomb as larger, deadlier, and more horribly vicious than any other bomb yet manufactured. But if it had been a big bomb, none of us would have breathed the peaceful air of spring in Hampshire that lunchtime.

After lunch, I telephoned the adjutant of my battalion. He was sympathetic, saying I could take my time about returning, and I sat back to enjoy two days' unexpected leave in the luxury of a private house and borrowed civilian clothes. At last I began to feel clean again. (One girl washed her hair seven times and the water still came out looking like a puddle on a road.) We talked a lot about what had happened. Every now and then there would sweep over me, without warning, an extraordinary sensation, exultant and yet fearful, at the realisation of my own good fortune. Every now and then, too, there would come a momentary return of the dull, aching depression I had felt just after the bomb fell.

I was convinced I had no other after-effects, that the whole thing was behind me and done with. But two days later this happened: my hostess rose to leave the dinner table. At the door she stopped at a switch, meaning to put out some of the lights. Accidentally she put them all out. She switched them on again the next second, but in that instant I was out of my chair in one scared bound. A girl, the only other person there who had been bombed with me, was on her feet too, clutching her napkin. I don't know precisely what sensation she had, but during that moment of darkness there came inexplicably to my nostrils a paralysing whiff of that unique smell.

8

OFFICE — WITH A BATH

IN A list of the rôles in life with which I would be most unlikely to be identified, 'popular educator' would have to be
given a high place—up there with, say, racing motorist,
nuclear physicist, Master of Foxhounds, or night club
bouncer. Yet, I suppose, 'popular educator' was the basic
function of anybody who was a founder-member of the
staff of the Army Bureau of Current Affairs. I had, of course,
no idea what I was in for when this assignment came my
way; it made me an officer of the General Staff for some
months and though I did not last long I must say in defence
that I left of my own accord and not, as might well be
imagined, by popular demand.

As high and far as I can go in tracing the genesis of this
revolutionary idea in the British Army is to the Adjutant-
General, then General Sir Ronald Adam. The chain of
causation from him to me, a junior infantry officer in the
field, was curious and, like so many things in the Army,
fortuitous. The AG delegated the creation of this new
bureau to the Directorate of Education and Welfare, headed
by a lively young Major-General named Harry Willans (he
was still under fifty when he died in an air crash in the Middle
East). As the cornerstone of ABCA was to be publications
for circulation throughout the Army, General Willans decided he needed some journalists. He asked the then
Director of Public Relations at the War Office (Ian Hay, the
novelist) if he had any such creatures up his sleeve and the
DPR, no doubt rummaging around in the trays, found a

memorandum to his predecessor from the Parliamentary Secretary to the Secretary of State for War which referred to me.

To jump to the other end of the chain, what had happened was that a friend of mine had met me on leave while I was a corporal in searchlights and had decided flatteringly that I was being wasted. My friend took this up with a friend of his, Jim Thomas (the late Lord Cilcennen), who was Anthony Eden's Parliamentary Secretary. Hence the memo.

The result was that I returned from leave to my battalion to be told casually by the Adjutant that a message had come in about me—'some dogsbody job at the War House' was how he described it, I recall. I reported at one of the hotels in Northumberland Avenue which had become War Office annexes and found myself with two other officers similarly summoned, Bevil Rudd and Anthony Cotterell. Rudd was the eldest and most senior; his connection with journalism was peripheral, for he had been a celebrated runner and had written on athletics in a morning newspaper. Cotterell I knew on nodding terms, for he had been on the *Daily Express* before the war when I was working on the *Sunday Express*, two floors above, and we used to meet in the lift.

We were summoned to General Willans, who delighted me by working in his braces, which was unlike what I expected at the War Office, and was much given to the expression that something wasn't worth 'two pennyworth of cold gin'. Every time he said it, which was at least daily, I had a shuddering thought of how nasty warm gin would be. The General told us we *were*, for the moment, the Army Bureau of Current Affairs, but we would soon be joined by a civilian boss—Emlyn Williams. This surprised me, but as I knew Emlyn I looked forward to his arrival. A few days later the new boss arrived and turned out to be William

Emrys Williams (now Sir, and Secretary-General of the Arts Council), a much more likely appointment, for he was, unlike the rest of us, a popular educator by training and experience.

It was decided that ABCA should start with a weekly, or two alternating fortnightly, publications and we were allocated offices with a simple yet alarming brief—to think. Cotterell and I shared a room high up in the hotel, with a private bathroom attached. It had the regulation furniture: two desks, four chairs, table and a filing cabinet, and that was all. We were invited to summon secretarial assistance as required from the typing pool.

Cotterell, a practical man, produced his own portable typewriter and got on with the book he was writing about his experiences as a recruit. He was essentially a writer, and such things as editing and layout were of no interest to him. For myself, I doodled away with coloured pencils and printers' type-specimen books, lists of subject-ideas, and possible authors, to produce a suggested format and contents for our publications.

Williams was busy on a higher level and a grander scale, planning the Bureau as a whole. It was the soldier Willans and the civilian Williams who put the ABCA idea on the level where it became an order in the Army and not just one of those welfare 'facilities' which were offered and as often as not ignored. ABCA was a 'must'. It was because of Williams' knowledge of 'discussion techniques' that our publications, *War* and *Current Affairs*, were not things to be read or skimmed and discarded, but were official handbooks on which officers had to act. Later in the war—and after it—I met officers who scowled when they learned that I had been one of the people behind those 'ABCA periods' which were forced on them.

Cotterell and I decided on the title *War*, and I drew its glaring red and white cover. Also, while doodling away

107

those warm summer afternoons, I devised the beehive-shaped monogram of the letters ABCA which became our trademark. Cotterell was emphatic that our first publication should be called *War* because it afforded the opportunity to answer the telephone with the words 'This is *War*', which are susceptible of a variety of dramatic enunciations.

Apart from the day-to-day work of editing, my contributions to ABCA were so few that I can remember them distinctly. Nobody is ever really grateful for a saving of the taxpayers' money but I was quietly pleased when I had the notion that the ABCA wall-maps should carry a black-and-white picture feature on the back so that when a new up-to-date map was issued the old one could be reversed and have another lease of life. But my principal achievement (and my only other) was my most unpopular. I asked one day if our publications were to carry dates and the answer was 'Yes'. I pointed out that few if any Army publications did, and the timing of their emergence was governed by the machinery of His Majesty's Stationery Office. If we carried a date, and our span of life was a week, we had to come out on time, and topicality was vital. Rightly, I was told to work this out for myself. On a couple of preliminary or dry-run issues I found my fears were well-founded. We were receiving proofs about twenty-four hours before publication date. A little investigation revealed a typical Civil Service bottleneck. The printers were under instructions to send the proofs to a civil department of the War Office, concerned with contracts, and there they were checked, at civil service pace, to ensure presumably that the War Office was getting what it was paying for.

This system was invariable, I was told. I went to see an official at the Stationery Office. I knew the moment I entered the room that I was at a disadvantage. Every civil service rank has a military equivalent and the man at the desk (I guessed and checked later) was about Brigadier level. He looked pointedly at my shoulder and I realised he resented dealing with mere captains. I put my case. It was stonily received. The procedure was normal and there should be no delay. But there *was* delay, I insisted; fatal delay. If I couldn't have the proofs more quickly then could I have a separate set for editorial purposes? No, that was impossible. It was one of those moments when it was useful to remember that you were in a job you couldn't be fired from. The worst that could be done to me was to be sent back to my regiment —and that was no punishment.

'Have you ever seen a proof pulled?' I asked.

I can't remember his exact words but they were intended to convey that my question was impertinent in the common and also the exact sense of the word. They also made it clear he had never seen a proof pulled.

'A printer takes a galley of type and lays it on a sort of table,' I said, with accompanying actions. 'Then he inks the type and then he puts a sheet of paper on top, presses a treadle and a roller runs over the paper, thereby making an inked impression of the type on the paper.'

Maybe this mounting impertinence—for I was talking as if to a backward child—made him speechless, but anyhow he said nothing.

'If that printer,' I added, 'presses that treadle twice instead of once our problem is solved.'

I was dismissed with a mumble about the matter being looked into, but from then on I received a set of proofs promptly from the printer, and dealt with them, and when the other set arrived a day or two later via the contract department I put them on a hook in the office and never looked at them. Any marks or comments on them certainly never reached the printer. In this way I may have fouled the pure channel of War Office procedure but our pamphlets came out on time and that was all I cared about.

If I was ignorant and graceless in matters of protocol and precedence Cotterell was much worse. He did what he wanted to do the way he wanted to do it and apologised afterwards if necessary. The trouble was that his apologies were so overdone, so studded with 'sirs' and self-abasement, that I was always sure the recipient was going to realise that the whole thing was an act and that in fact he was being ridiculed by this pale, straight-faced young man with the quiet voice.

Perhaps the best example of his technique happened before he came to ABCA. He told me the story when, somehow, the name of Colonel Bingham came up. The Colonel was a commandant of an Officer Cadet Training Unit who achieved brief fame early in the war with a letter to *The Times* which lauded the Old School Tie so far as officer candidates were concerned.

Fusilier Cotterell went to Colonel Bingham's unit about this time. He wanted to write an article for the *Daily Express* on the life of a cadet. He felt sure it would be difficult to get what he would write passed by the CO. So he wrote the article and the day it appeared in print he presented himself at his company office clutching a copy of the paper and doing his best to look pale and worried. Anthony was naturally pale and especially in battledress he looked disarmingly young and innocent.

He requested that the Sergeant-Major take him before the CO. The interview with the formidable Colonel Bingham went something like this:

AC. 'Sir, a terrible thing has happened.'

CO. 'Well, my boy, what is it?'

AC. (*rather breathlessly*) 'Sir—I was a journalist in civilian life. I wrote an article about officer training, sir, and I knew I had to submit it for you approval, sir.'

CO. 'Yes, my boy, quite right.'

AC. 'But, sir, I had no typewriter and my handwriting is

very bad, sir, and I did not want to waste your time, especially as the article might not be accepted. So I sent it to the paper, sir, with a letter saying if they wanted to use it would they send me a proof first so that I could submit it for your approval. But (*producing the paper*) look what they've done, sir. They've gone and printed it.'

I am sure that at this point Anthony sounded distraught at this heinous breach of King's Regulations into which his good intentions had led him. The response was exactly what he had foreseen. Colonel Bingham was fatherly, stern yet sympathetic. He knew what these newspapers were, he said; such behaviour was typical. He understood. In future if Cadet Cotterell thought of writing anything for the Press he should come and see him (the CO) first and he would give him the benefit of his advice.

And Cadet Cotterell, having said a fervent 'Thank you, sir,' marched out of the Orderly Room, exonerated without being charged, under the wing instead of the lash of the feared Colonel Bingham.

Attack, Anthony murmured, unoriginally but aptly, is the best defence.

But often he simply got away with his natural behaviour. The Adjutant-General was no stickler for formalities and he was keenly interested in ABCA's formative days. He telephoned General Willans one day and said, 'Send the chaps over.' It took Willans some time to realise that this meant his two ABCA staff captains. On one occasion he came straight through on the line to our room and asked for me. Cotterell answered, and he was busy.

'Sorry,' he said, without asking who was speaking, 'you can't. He's in the bath—thinking.' It was a hot afternoon and he was telling the truth. I was in a cool bath and I was supposed to be thinking. The AG fortunately thought it very funny.

III

So long as I was in ABCA I edited Anthony's copy. He professed to be grateful. When I left he did it rather better for himself. That was typical. It was a boring job, especially as his copy was always very messy, full of written-in emendations, balloons of insertions in the margins, and punctuation of a rather impressionistic sort. He loved to dump an article on my desk, the pages unclipped and disordered, the paper crumpled, and watch me wade through it, trying to make the printer's task more tolerable. Secretly, of course, he was laughing at my fussiness. He could do all that was needed with complete efficiency. But if there was somebody else to be got to do the boring job, then the obvious thing was to plead ignorance and let the fool do it.

His reports, not for publication but for our information on how ABCA was going, were always enjoyable. Once after a visit to a unit he ascribed the local mishandling of our great idea to a Commanding Officer whose 'social-political outlook was mid-way between the flat earth theory and Home Rule for Cornwall'.

Anthony's eye and ear for the significant line or moment were deadly. I formed the habit of asking him, when he returned from his reporting excursions for ABCA, if anything had happened that he had not written. Usually there was something. For example, when he came back from visiting one of the first US Army units to arrive in Britain he turned in an admirable story, informative, descriptive, amusing, just what was needed then to ensure that the British Army should learn about and understand its new ally. But he told me one item which he felt he could not write yet which summed up one of the rather startling differences of those days between the two Armies.

While he was being shown round by the second-in-command he was left for a moment in the lobby of the Officers' Mess. He had been told that the 'old man'—the CO—was a very fierce and stern character. A sergeant walked into the lobby and pinned a notice up on the board. Anthony strolled over and read:

'Officers are reminded to line up squaws for beer party Tuesday.'

At that moment the 'old man' came clumping down the stairs, looking fierce enough to justify his reputation. He strode over to the notice-board and read over Anthony's shoulder in silence. Anthony, already surprised by the tone of the notice, wondered what would happen. A little awed, he waited for the outburst. At last the Colonel spoke. 'Toosday, eh?' he murmured and walked away.

Sometimes in our early days of innocence about the War Office we were saved by kindly senior officers—usually regulars, whom I always found more helpful than the temporary sort. I was writing a brief minute in a file one day and my pen ran dry. I picked up the nearest thing to my hand which was a red-ink pen. A day or two later a full staff colonel in another directorate telephoned and said he had read my minute with interest. Was I, he asked softly with a hint of a chuckle, by any chance familiar with a volume with some such title as War Office Rules? I said no, I had never heard of it. He recommended me to a certain section, sub-section and paragraph. I sent for the book and found that it clearly laid down that minutes would be written in red only by the Secretary of State for War. I telephoned my kind friend. He had my minute typed and pasted over the original, and blacked in my signature.

ABCA was soon adjudged to be a success, whatever the man in the ranks (or his officer) may have thought about it, and we began to grow. All the main lines of our operation were set and, under the strong but light-reined hand of Bill Williams, everything was running smoothly. More and more Cotterell became the star writer and I the editor. Rudd was the contact man. He seemed to know everybody, be known and liked everywhere, and he was wonderfully persuasive. Time and again we had an idea which was fine except that we were sure nobody would play—that is, we required co-operation at a level which even we in our brashness didn't know how to reach. We would mention it to Rudd, he would take somebody to lunch and the doors were open to us.

I had the simple notion that we might run in *War* a feature called 'The Story Behind the Medal'; the stories themselves would be exciting reading and we might spread the idea that even winners of the VC were quite ordinary fellows and not heroic freaks. Rudd tackled somebody in the Military Secretary's office and I was given access to the files on awards. The first VC file I read was one of the most dramatic documents I have ever handled. It began with a recommendation in the field scribbled on a scrap of paper. As it passed up the line of command it dropped—by recommendation—to a DCM and then to an MM, then up again to VC, and there it stayed. The penultimate document was signed by the King. Last of all was a prosaic letter to a firm of jewellers on the lines of 'Please engrave one Victoria Cross . . .'

But our growth had an unfortunate result—at least so Cotterell and I thought. I don't think I am insulting anybody when I say that for a considerable time ABCA was the only part of Army Education that was lively and meant anything. The officers of the Army Education Corps, of which I had never previously heard, began to move in on us. Here was a Good Thing, they had obviously decided. These textbook evangelists, worthy and erudite characters no doubt, were as remote from the ordinary soldier as the man in the moon. Cotterell and I were not dons, nor even schoolmasters; not even really very well educated; and we were journalists with a background in popular newspapers.

But we had both served in the ranks and as infantry subalterns and we knew how soldiers ticked.

Williams was for us and we could have survived, but I began to see a faint red light and to consider what my next move
should be. I wrote to a friend who was by then commanding
a battalion of my regiment, asking if it might be arranged for
me to join him. I was uneasily conscious that the war had
now been going on for nearly three years and, while I had
been in the Army since the day it began, a shallow ellipse
drawn around London, touching Wiltshire on one side and
the East Coast on the other, would cover the area of my
service. Economically too it was time I moved away from
London. My total pay and allowances were about eight
pounds a week, on which I had to house and feed myself,
and I had, I confess, slipped back into some of the peacetime habits of bachelor life which had long been based on an
income several times larger.

But before I could take any independent action a swift
transformation took place in circumstances which are better
described separately and I found myself an Intelligence
Officer—and still in London.

Cotterell stayed on with ABCA when I left, but he went
his own way, even more independently; he was too valuable
to be interfered with and a difficult man to gainsay. Somehow, gradually, he worked things, including promotion to
major, so that he became a correspondent in the Army for
the Army, telling ordinary men what other ordinary men
were doing. He went off and qualified as a parachutist
without telling anybody. He made unofficial but useful contacts with the RAF and the US Air Force and flew many
times over enemy territory. These adventures he reported
in the ABCA pamphlets in a way which made the reader
understand and even feel what it was like to do such things.
Some of these articles he reprinted in what was, unfortunately, his last book, *An Apple for the Sergeant*, which

completed the trilogy he began so successfully as a conscript recruit with *What! No Morning Tea?*

Cotterell was only twenty-six when he died, in 1944, after parachuting into Arnhem with the 1st Airborne Division. After a long period when he was listed as missing it was reported that he had been wounded and when the evacuation took place had been left behind in the hands of German army doctors. Months later he came into the charge of SS men and it is believed that he was shot 'in circumstances amounting to a war crime'.

9

COMMANDO

ON THE railings outside a building in a quiet cul-de-sac off Whitehall during the war there hung a board on which was painted 'Reserved for CCO's Car'. On the building itself was another board which read 'Combined Operations HQ'.

The officer who parked in that space was the then Vice-Admiral Lord Louis Mountbatten (also Honorary Lieut.-General and Air Marshal), Chief of Combined Operations. That made him (among other things) the head man of the Commandos.

The Commandos had been in existence as part of the British Army for about eight months before they seeped through into print. That was in March 1941, and the name Commando had not yet been resurrected from the Boer War to pass into popular usage. The earliest clipping I can trace simply records the formation of a *corps d'élite*, picked from the whole Army, to be trained with unprecedented rigorousness for purposes unspecified.

The public heard little more on the subject until October. Then came a sudden broadside of Commando news. On October 11 every newspaper carried substantially the same story, not unnaturally as it was a hand-out from Combined Operations HQ. Pendant to this general piece about the Commandos and the type of training they were doing was a brief news story, telling how the King had lately stood 'on the shores of a remote Scottish loch' and watched Commando men demonstrate their skill in landing aggressively from assault craft.

117

At this time the name 'Commando' was born and credit for it is generally given to the Prime Minister, Winston Churchill. Adding his natural flair for the apt colour-word, and the fact that he was a front-line war correspondent when the South African Commandos were big news, the PM's baptism of these irregular, self-supporting units is more than likely.

A few weeks later Admiral of the Fleet Sir Roger Keyes announced in Parliament that his office of Director of Combined Operations had been withdrawn from him on October 19 by the Chiefs of Staff Committee. It was only when he was out of the job that the public learned for the first time that he had been in. He had, he said, held the office for fifteen months, which places the birth of the Commandos around July 1940, or just after Dunkirk.

Press and public interest in Commandos was lively. Here were action troops: the implications of a new striking force, trained to land on foreign shores in special boats, were manna to all the 'invade the Continent' wishful-thinkers of the period. Editors who had long known that such bodies existed followed up these first releases like dogs off a leash. So the publicity was profuse. Most of it was intensely disliked by the Commando men of all ranks. Typical was a Sunday paper's two-page feature, headed 'The Toughest Men on Earth' in inch-high capitals. That sort of thing made the Commandos wince and groan. Stories like that, they felt, had a two-fold unfortunate result. The public misunderstood the Commandos, over-glamourised them and thought of them as dare-devil cut-throats. The rest of the Army misunderstood them, because it pictured them as swaggering, undisciplined tough guys, over-publicised and over-privileged. (It was a common fallacy among soldiers that Commandos got extra pay and never did any parades.)

A letter signed 'Plain English Soldier' appeared in a London newspaper beginning: 'May I endorse the resentment many of us feel about the use of the term Commando? Who are these men . . .?'

To provide an answer to that last question was clearly the sort of thing the Army Bureau of Current Affairs existed to do, and the assignment fell to me. There were some preliminary difficulties when I started negotiations to penetrate the tight little world of the Commandos, but once my purpose was understood I had all the co-operation I wanted.

My first journey was to Scotland, to see the Brigadier, the immediate superior of the Lieutenant-Colonel who commanded each Commando. I arrived the night before the interview and stayed in the same hotel as most of the officers on the Brigade Staff. They were few and all had served in the Commandos themselves; there were none of the conventional desk-anchored 'staff jobs' in this outfit. Each officer believed the Commando he came from to be the best, and inter-Commando rivalry made any 'shop' discussion healthily combative. Where all united was in general pro-Commando fervour.

As the Brigadier wouldn't be back till morning, I sat around after dinner with the only staff officer who was free that evening. He was indulging in his only relaxation, *The Times* crossword puzzle, and I think I won his gratitude by helping him with one or two clues that worried him. When that was done I persuaded him to talk Commandos, and clarified and confirmed one or two preliminary points for myself. First, every man in the Commandos was a volunteer and came from an ordinary regiment, where he had already become a trained soldier. Nobody could join the Commandos from civilian life, neither by volunteering nor on conscription. Second, a Commando as a formation was different in structure from any other Army unit. The proportion of available fighting men was higher in a Commando than elsewhere, and indeed every man was a fighting man, for the few who worked as clerks, drivers, etc., all had to measure up to the general standard of fitness and skill at arms, and take time out regularly from their sedentary jobs to keep their hands in as all-round soldiers.

I cleared up too the question of money. Commando pay was ordinary Army pay according to rank. Where mis-understanding had arisen was over the living-out system on which the Commandos worked. The men were neither billeted nor fed by the Army. Instead, each man received an allowance of six shillings and eightpence a day with which he had to house and feed himself. With the appetite-creating work the Commandos did and the high war-time cost of living there was no margin here. The sum was a computa-tion, translated into civilian terms, of what it cost the Army to maintain a soldier.

The allowance was withheld for any day the man was not paying his own way. Thus, each time a Commando went on an operation against the enemy (such as a raid on the enemy-occupied coast) the men lost their allowance.

This living-out system was one of the bases of the whole Commando idea. Regular Army officers who came into the Commandos at the beginning frankly admitted they were sceptical. They thought the system would be fatal to discipline. There would be no lights-out time, no check-up to ensure every man was in. How could a body of men be controlled if, after working hours, they were scattered all over a town, in lodgings wherever their fancy took them? How would men get on parade in time in the morning with no sergeant to roar hell and destruction all round the barrack room at reveille?

Soon the same officers swore by the system. There were no late-comers on parade. 'Crime' was remarkably low. The men kept good hours. The officers explained this by saying that with the right men what amounts to an honour system works better than compulsion and close supervision. If a Commando soldier found a good billet he was treated as one of the family. He enjoyed that. The householder was under no compulsion to keep him, so he behaved himself if he wanted to stay. Most of the homes in which the men lodged had a parent-made rule about when the front door was locked. The soldier toed the line.

The best reason for the general absence of punishable offences in the Commandos was a simple one. The punishment was liable to be one unknown to military law but well-known to the Commando soldier as 'RTU'. It meant Return to Unit. It was the punishment he feared most— being turned out of the Commandos.

This punishment was a powerful weapon in the hands of a Commanding Officer. He could send any officer or man back to his unit at any time without giving a reason. Similarly he never had to accept in his Commando any man of any rank if he did not want him. This, of course, gave the Commando a hand-picked character. The CO had to like you, respect your skill as a soldier, want to have you. Otherwise you'd be on the train at a moment's notice—RTU.

Another staff captain came into the hotel lounge. He had gone back to work after dinner and it was now nearly midnight. He had to wait up to receive an officer who was driving about a hundred miles with a message that would have to be dealt with on arrival. We settled down with a glass of beer and he told me that he had recently conducted an interview for a batch of Commando volunteers. There were thirty-eight at the start, all men who had come up before their regimental Commanding Officers as Commando applicants and had been approved to go forward.

The Commando officer—sometimes it is one of the Colonels looking for likely men for his own unit—first of all outlined to them the nature of the service for which they were volunteering. This had been found necessary because so many men came up with wrong ideas. Some had heard

121

about the living-out system, and dreamt of feather beds and home comforts. The officer explained that the standards of fitness and efficiency were high, the discipline strict, and the training far more strenuous than anything they had known before. The jobs they would get would be dangerous and they would carry their lives in their hands all the time. If a 'suicide squad' job came along there would be no call for volunteers. It would be assumed that every man was ready for anything.

After this little speech he gave them ten minutes to think it over and back out if they felt like it. When he called for them one by one twenty-eight men presented themselves. Of these he chose eighteen, with some doubtfuls among them. To the others he said, 'Sorry,' because on a few minutes' private conversation it seemed to him that their standard of training, temperament, and personality fell short of requirements.

Then the Medical Officer went over the eighteen carefully and weeded out seven more. All these men were medically in the top grade, or they would not have been allowed to come forward, but Commando standards had to be exceptionally high. Both at the medical examinations and the personal interviews it was often the big muscular man who was eliminated. Sometimes he failed to show the mental alertness required; sometimes his physique was illusory, and his stamina likely to be lower than that of the less impressive, more 'average' type. The selecting officer now had eleven men—eight certains and three doubtfuls who confessed that they could not swim. He accepted them all for training at least. The three non-swimmers learned, and all eleven were admitted to the Commando ranks.

Next morning I visited Brigade Headquarters and asked the Brigadier if he could give me a one-sentence definition of a Commando.

'I could write you a book about it,' he said, 'but I doubt if

I could get it into one sentence.' He looked thoughtful for a minute, and then speaking slowly, said this:

'A Commando is a group of men trained in amphibious warfare, and prepared to carry out tasks in which in almost every case the successful outcome depends upon high skill at arms, speed, silence, field-craft, discipline and initiative.'

It is noticeable that apart from the word 'amphibious' that definition should be applicable to any group of fighting soldiers. That is a point the Commando men were anxious to emphasise. They *were* normal soldiers. They were banded together to carry out special tasks which required special training, but they were neither freaks nor supermen. I also asked the Brigadier to sum up what he thought the specialised Commando training achieved. Again he replied, slowly and thoughtfully, and I wrote down what he said:

'The existence of Commandos has given an opportunity not available before for soldiers to study sailors and sailors to study soldiers—to get to know each other, to learn something about each other's work, and to respect one another. Both have learned a lot.'

When I was packing my bag to move on to a Commando stationed some miles away I was telephoned by one of the Brigade staff, who told me that I could catch the COs of two Commandos at the same place that afternoon, as their units were playing rugby together. It was a bitterly cold day, with snow lying thick on the high ground, and the roads like frosted mirrors, but when I arrived at the football ground I found I was the only man wearing a greatcoat. All the soldiers on the touch-lines were wearing sleeveless jerkins, finishing above the knee and tied round the waist with rope. Commando soldiers never wore greatcoats. It may have been partly pose to begin with, but they said they found they could work more freely in the less conventional garb. The ropes used as belts were part of Commando equipment and the invention of a Commando officer. In the

123

Norway campaign, where a good many of the Commando men were in the Independent Companies, a hazardous river crossing was made by means of rifle slings joined together. The inventive officer decided to go one better and make it unnecessary in such cases for the men to remove their slings. The result was an issue to every man of a six-foot length of rope, about half-inch thick, with a five-inch wooden bar at one end and a loop at the other. They were called toggle-and-eye ropes, and they had many uses. The Commandos had a drill for making a toggle bridge, which was roughly hammock-shaped, and from the moment a troop arrived at a river until they were all across and the bridge dismantled the time was twenty-five minutes. The bridge was thirty-three feet long, and the first two men swam across with it.

There was one man on the rugby field who seemed to be doing a terrific job of rallying, encouraging, and directing his team as well as playing a strenuous game. He looked a shade older than the others and when he came off the field he was introduced as the Colonel commanding one of the units. He was a civil engineer in civilian life, still in his thirties, and fanatically keen on his job. Most of the Commando Colonels were regular soldiers, however, but the average age was round about the forty mark, and only one or two saw service in the first World War.

We went along to the tea-room of a local ice rink after the match, and both teams sat down to tea, officers and men mixing freely and easily. I sat with the two Colonels and their seconds-in-command. Sometimes when I asked a question they debated their answers in the light of their individual methods, making it obvious that in running the Commandos a great deal was left to the man on the spot in the application of general instructions from above, with the result that each Commando had a distinct character of its own, evolved and conditioned by the personality of the men in charge. But their general experiences were the same. Both enthused about the living-out system as a means of developing self-discipline which they regarded as the basis of Commando life. Both found that the most useful man was an average sort of fellow, with no sensational physique but with a lot of common sense, an active sense of humour, and a keenness on his job strong enough to be proof against all inconveniences, discomforts, and disappointments.

The least useful man, they found, was the 'pub brawler' type, who is belligerent twenty-four hours a day. This fellow would inevitably rise to the bait often dangled before Commando soldiers in public places. It consisted of a soldier of another unit, usually having had a few drinks, coming up and saying aggressively: 'What's so tough about you Commando guys? I'll take you on any time.' The Commando 'undesirable', if he had not been found out already, would land himself in a fight, the penalty for which was almost inevitably RTU. The sensible Commando man either turned the situation into a joke or turned on his heel and walked away.

Talking of the ability of Commando soldiers to think and fend for themselves, one Colonel told me that he was once ordered to move to a town 120 miles away. The Army Transport authorities telephoned him and asked what train arrangements would be required. 'None,' he said. When the men were dismissed that afternoon they were told that next morning's parade would be at X, thirty miles away. No further explanation was given and no questions were asked. Every man was on parade at the right place at the right time. Nobody cared how he got there. Then the Commando marched the remaining ninety miles to its new station.

Later that evening I had a drink with one of the Colonels and his team. There was no awkwardness about who should treat whom. Every man, from Colonel to private, contributed to a pool, from which the drinks (beer all round) were bought. I asked if, in view of the high standard of physical fitness maintained, any of the men had given up such weaknesses of the flesh as drinking and smoking. The answer was 'Definitely not'. The average man in the Commandos smoked and drank in moderation, just as he did before the war. There was one case of a heavy smoker being sent back to his unit—but not just because he was a heavy smoker. He had a smoker's cough which betrayed him on night exercises. It was suggested that if he eased off his smoking the cough might go. He did not make the effort, and he went.

There was a good deal of noise coming from a room in the hotel where I was staying, and the Colonel took me along. It was a farewell party to a troop commander who had been posted to a new job. Most of the men had been with him since the Norway campaign, and their grief at his going was obviously sincere. I left the Colonel playing 'South of the Border' on the piano, while the men crowded round and sang.

Next morning, the second-in-command took me out to see some training in progress. He was a little concerned lest the democratic gaiety of the previous night's party had given me a wrong impression, so he insisted that I should see the troop concerned at work. They were on a field exercise, attacking a railway bridge held by some of their own men, and it was easy to reassure him that they looked as efficient and well-disciplined as if they had been tucked up in bed early the night before.

There was only one demonstration staged for my benefit. The second-in-command called for two men to be sent to him. I had plenty of opportunity to convince myself that they were picked at random. When they came into the room he laid a map in front of them, pointed with his finger and said:—'We're here. Look at the village of "Z", eight miles south. I may want to send a troop there. Go and look at the place, find out the facilities for accommodation, ground for training, a hall for lectures, games fields, and so on. Let me have your report by 1600 hours.' It was then about 11 a.m. The men asked no questions, saluted, and went off.

Some days after I returned to London I received their report by post. It certainly covered all the prescribed ground, down to the fact that the owner of a local hall was willing to lend it without charge.

We went to the riverside where a numbing snow-wind was blowing in from the sea. About thirty coatless soldiers were practising putting off from a jetty in a row-boat. To my landsman's eye they looked as expert as sailors. It was an essential of Combined Operations that soldiers should be able to understand and act on orders from naval officers, and the sergeant in charge of this party was rapping out instructions mysterious to me, but with which they seemed completely at home. There was a system of co-operation with the Navy by which a Commando troop would go off for several weeks at a time and live on board ship, taking their share of the duties and familiarising themselves with naval routine. One senior officer said to me, 'When we began, the sailors were apt to look on themselves as ferrymen for us, and the soldiers were apt to be passengers and nothing more. Now they are all fighting men together.'

A glance through some specimen training programmes in the Colonel's office made it clear that the Commando's claim to be normal soldiers was well founded. And they *did* have drill parades. One training instruction read: 'Drill parades of short duration will be included in normal daily routine. The parade, not longer than half an hour, will be intense, and every man, including the instructor, must be at maximum pressure.' Once, when a visiting high officer was known to have inspected the ceremonial guard mounting of a Guards Battalion the previous day, a Commando put on their own guard mounting just to show that they could do the ceremonial stuff as well as anybody.

127

One of the ways in which a Commando differed from other units was that there were no cooks on the strength. But every man had to know something about cooking as a part of his self-maintenance in the field. Often, on exercises, arrangements were made for the purchase of live sheep from farms en route, and these were given to the men to be killed and cooked. Every man had instructions in the rudiments of field butchery as well as open-air cooking.

Though the kind of tasks Commandos went in for pre-supposed their landing and fighting on foot, they were all taught to drive anything on wheels or tracks, motor-boats and even railway engines. They had artillery instruction so that they knew what to do with a field gun if they captured one, either to put it out of or into action. They knew sema-phore and morse and could operate a radio transmitter set. They learned German phrases and practised on one another.

Sometimes they did things which made it reasonable for outsiders to look on them as tough guys. One Commando had two days off duty at Christmas, but the third day they had a 'sweat parade' involving physical training, cross-country running, and a sea bathe. They recommended the routine as the perfect pick-me-up after holiday indulgence.

One of the stories told in the newspapers to emphasise the superman qualities which the Commandos denied possessing, was of the time when a Commando marched sixty-seven-and-a-half miles in a day. A Major who took part in this march was at pains to explain that it was done for medical experi-mental purposes. The actual marching time was seventeen and a half hours, and the longest halt was an hour, in which a meal was eaten. Seventy per cent of the men finished the course, but that does not mean that thirty per cent dropped by the wayside. Any man showing signs of distress was ordered out by the doctors for examination.

The normal Commando marching speed was three and a

half miles an hour for distances up to twenty miles. For occasions when speed was required, they had a table which ranged from seven miles in one hour (run-march) to twelve miles in three hours. When endurance was the test the standard was thirty-five miles in fourteen hours. Once a Commando, practising living on the country, spent two days marching sixty miles to take part in a large-scale manoeuvre. This lasted two days, and when it was over they marched the sixty miles home again. Throughout, they bivouacked by night. Commando bivouacking was not the old improvised blanket-tent arrangement. Experienced at digging themselves in cosily, they combined shelter with concealment in various ingenious structures of earth and foliage.

The Commandos had nothing against their exploits being described to the public, and most of them had newspaper cuttings about such operations as Vaagso, Lofoten, Bardia, Syria, and other items which went to make the brief eventful history of Commandos in action up to that time. These were read eagerly by the men who were not in the shows themselves, and they didn't even try to conceal their jealousy. Where they put the publicity barrier up was against the sensational 'personal adventure' story. Most of these, they claimed, were obtained by reporters from landladies to whom the soldier-lodgers had yarned fancifully on their return in an amiable endeavour to maintain secrecy and at the same time satisfy curiosity round the tea table.

One troop I visited were still chuckling over a Vaagso incident in which one of their comrades was involved. This man had a passion for souvenirs. At Vaagso he was ordered to double across a gap under enemy fire, between two houses. As he doubled he noticed a German steel helmet lying half-hidden on the ground. In his stride he reached over to lift it. It did not come away and he pulled harder. The face of a very frightened German soldier came into view.

129

Another story from Norway was of a German officer who came forward smiling, with his hands up. 'Thank God, that's me out of the German Army,' he said, in fluent if not quite grammatical English. He was an opera singer who had travelled widely and appeared frequently in England, but happened to be at home when the war came.

10

LEADERS OF MEN

WHEN I first saw soldiers being scientifically tested for their suitability as officers my reaction was intense relief that I had been commissioned before all this began. Back in *my* day, some three years earlier, an officer was chosen from the ranks by a series of brief, often somewhat nebulous interviews with his superiors.

In my own case, I was summoned to Battalion Headquarters, marched into the Colonel's office and told that in a few minutes I would be presented to the Brigade Commander as one of the Colonel's candidates for a commission. A form filled in with particulars about me lay before the Colonel and he checked this over, more to rehearse the details, I felt, than anything else. (His knowledge of me at first hand was restricted to two or three meetings when my contribution consisted largely of 'Yes, sir' and 'No, sir'.) At the bottom of the form he scribbled a few words which, by squinting and neck-craning, I found to be 'Quick promotion in the field—fully justified'. This charming flattery appeared under the printed heading 'Recommendation'.

The interview with the Brigadier was short and pleasant. To the stock question 'Why do you want to be an officer?' I gave the conventionally correct reply—'Because I think I am capable of leading men.' (A man I know replied 'Because life's a great deal more comfortable', and his commission was delayed several months.)

A few days later I had to go to a town some miles away and see another Colonel. I had opted for a commission in another arm of the service—the infantry—so I had to be approved by a senior infantry officer. This was a curious interview. The Colonel had never seen me in his life before and it was improbable that he ever would again.

He had my recommendation form before him and as he ran over the items—not so much questioning me as saying things like 'So you've been eight months in the Army, have you?' and 'A journalist, eh? That must be interesting'—I had a feeling that he didn't quite know what to say. When he had exhausted the conversational leads offered by the form he looked up sharply and said in a much livelier tone, 'What games do you play?' I had seen enough of the British Regular Army to know that the simple, truthful answer 'None' was unlikely to do me good. With what I realise now was probably a revolting, false-modest, ingratiating smile, I replied, 'I'm a Scotsman, sir. All Scotsmen play golf.' In truth, my passion for the game had barely survived my teens and when I moved from Scotland to London I gave my clubs to my sister and never bothered to buy another set; I had not seen a ball struck, far less struck one, for at least seven years.

The Colonel's face lit up. He was a keen golfer. Continuing my nauseating humility, I quickly established that while of course I had been born with a niblick in my hand, my opinion of my own prowess was low, partly because I had seen so much great golf in my life. As I hoped, this intrigued him and for the remainder of the interview I told him stories of Walter Hagen, Bobby Jones, Gene Sarazen *et al*, whom I had seen as a golf reporter. We parted cordially and soon afterwards I passed into an Officer Cadet Training Unit for my four months' officer-training.

All this, it will be seen, was rather casual and haphazard. Some unsuitable people got to OCTUs and the casualty rate was high. This caused wastage. If a third of the cadets enrolled at an OCTU were branded with the dread letters

132

RTU (Return to Unit) the output of officers for that period was only two-thirds of what it should have been, or a difference over the year of several thousand officers. Moreover, a cadet's life was overshadowed by this black cloud, RTU. I ticked off the days of my sixteen weeks like a convict and my relief when I stumbled out with a star on my shoulder was pathetic. I emerged more like a reprieved man than a confident leader.

Before long, however, the primitive method of selecting officers was changed, largely through the military psychiatrists, whose influence had been steadily growing in Army life. Psychological techniques were applied to recruits to discover their natural aptitudes and to soldiers considered by their commanders to be misfits or 'problems'. But it was in the process of officer selection that the psychological approach produced the most revolutionary changes.

There were soon scattered about Britain a number of Selection Boards and to these Commanding Officers sent their potential officers. I spent a couple of days at one of the Boards and saw a batch of thirty-nine candidates go through their tests. I was a captain by this time and the idea was that I should write a pamphlet explaining the work of the Selection Boards to the Army at large.

The Board I visited was operating at a fine old English country house not far from London and the setting was not at all accidental. The candidates arrived at lunch time and were shown to comfortable quarters, then to an ante-room and Mess certainly as good as they would be likely to find as officers; they were waited on by ATS girls and they had the run of the gardens and estate in their free time. The officers of the Selection Board staff mixed and ate with them and this opportunity to see the men under normal social conditions was a deliberate part of the scheme.

Each man on arrival was issued with two yellow, numbered armbands and for the next forty-eight hours he was

133

addressed by that number. The first afternoon was taken up with a series of fairly standard psychological tests.

The first test was a non-verbal one, more or less independent of education. The candidate was presented with a book, each page of which carried a problem. These were divided into sections and each group was progressively more difficult. For example, on one page a patterned square was printed and in the middle of the pattern there was a gap. At the bottom of the page were various fragments each of which would fit the gap for size and shape, but each carried a different pattern. The problem was to pick the fragment which would complete the design. That one was easy, but the designs became more complicated. In each case a sequence of thought was required to fill the gap. Plenty of time was allowed for this test. I ran through it myself and the psychiatrist who was with me estimated I would have scored about sixty per cent, or all right. Below fifty per cent was rather bad. The rare candidate who scored ninety per cent or over was showing signs of exceptional mental agility.

To check against this test there was one concerned with words and figures. Here there was a tight time limit. An elementary example question would be: 'If six is more than four write down eight; if not write down nine'. Or THRUSH is to COMMON as DODO is to CURIOUS, EXTINCT, AFRICAN, PARK, AUK. The idea has since become common, and is now applied to much lower age levels. Other tests were concerned with word-association and 'thematic apperception', in other words the candidate had to write a little story around a still picture projected on to a screen.

I saw the candidates' papers on these tests when they had completed them and gone to tea. They then came into the hands of a Sergeant Tester, an ex-schoolmaster who had lectured on psychology at his university. He was really a sieve for the psychiatrist who hadn't time to interview all

134

the men, but concentrated on those recommended by the Sergeant Tester as problems or doubtfuls.

I looked through some of the papers and made notes to watch out for certain candidates whose answers and reactions interested me. There was, for instance, the man to whom the word 'choke' suggested 'a gas-filled room'. (To most men this word conjured up hand-to-hand fighting, poison gas, or throttling an automobile engine.) To the same man 'strike' brought forth 'somebody being hit', which struck me as a curiously passive reaction for a fighting man. We will call him No. 11, and return to him later.

In the meantime the candidates had had a short talk from the President of the Board, a non-psychiatric Colonel, chosen for his all-round knowledge and experience of men and war. The Colonel told them about the course, pointed out that for the moment the nineteen-year-old private was equal to the sergeant-major with twenty years' service, and generally put the men at their ease. Then they were finished for the day, except that they dined with the staff and were no doubt conscious that impressions of them were being formed. This produced the two obvious extreme reactions—the man who tried to make an impression and the man stricken dumb with self-consciousness. The sensible man did his damnedest to be himself.

Next morning the men split into three parties of thirteen and a Military Testing Officer took charge of each for the day's work. I joined a Group Discussion. The testing officer threw to the class the then meaty subject of a Second Front. Volunteers were plentiful. What the speaker had to say was of secondary importance to how he said it. There was the stammerer, the ordinary half-shy man who got out what he had to say and gladly sat down, the more articulate man who made his points neatly in order, and, of course, the embryonic demagogue. The last interested me most. He got to his feet with a mock-humble murmur, 'Well, sir, if I may say a few words . . .', but before long he was brandishing his fist, leaning forward to his audience, playing organ-stop tricks with his voice, and using such phrases as 'And let me give you a word of warning, gentlemen,' and 'Let us see to it, each and every one of us.' I made a note to keep an eye on him. He was No. 23.

From there I went to the obstacle course, located in a clearing in a wood about two hundred yards from the house. The candidates, now changed into gym kit and rubber shoes, were assembled close to the course but out of sight of it, and told, in detail, what lay ahead of them. It was emphasised that they would find their way round the course by keeping between signs of two colours—blue on the left, red on the right. Then the whistle blew and the first man started. He came down a bank and found himself facing a goal-post structure with a double crossbar in the middle of which a small square was marked off with two short vertical bars, one blue, one red. Obviously he had to get through the square. He could jump up and catch the lower crossbar and swing himself through, he could climb one of the uprights, or he could use a rope which was lying handy. Which he chose was a matter of considerable interest to the testing officer who stood in the middle of the arena with a chart in his hand.

The candidate then followed the colours to a log wall about twelve feet high, which he had to climb. He circled the edge of the clearing until he came to a log which ran out from a bank to join a tree at a point about ten feet off the ground, where a wire hawser was slung to another tree about twenty yards away. The log brought a different reaction from practically every man. One ran along it with natural assurance. A second walked it like a tight-rope. Another walked a little, then sat down astride and drew himself along in an awkward series of bumps. The wire had to be walked too, but a handrope was provided, and the main

136

differences here were in the pace of progress. At the end of the wire the testee faced a vertical loose rope hung from an upper branch about six feet from him. He had to jump and catch this and, as it swung, drop to the ground beyond a given point. There was no physical difficulty in this.

After I had watched a few candidates I wondered if I was judging unfairly from the ground. Some men came along the wire and jumped almost without stopping. Others stood for a moment and obviously braced themselves. Others again hesitated longer and required more bracing. A very few smiled, shook their heads, and said they couldn't make it. I decided to try for myself. I was wearing uniform, street shoes, belt, cap, etc., but I found no difficulty except that my smooth leather soles were apt to slip on the wire, which slowed me down. Viewing the jump from this angle, it seemed to me apparent that if I merely fell forward and stretched out my arms I was bound to reach the rope. I did. My cap flew off as I swung to the ground but that was the only mishap I suffered. After that I judged the timorous more harshly.

The remaining two obstacles were a ditch, ten feet wide, which had to be crossed by a rope slung on to a horizontal branch and a fence like a badminton net which had to be cleared without touching it, jumping disallowed. This involved building some sort of rough structure from the materials lying about, such as forked logs, and in both tests the point was to see how much practical ingenuity the man possessed and if he learned from attempts that failed.

My demagogic friend No. 23 came through the obstacle course while I was there. He ran right into the middle of the arena, looking alert and vigorous, but entirely overlooking the colour guides. He blundered at every obstacle, grinned at his own errors, swore loudly, several times broke bounds by failing to follow the colours and revealed a strange inability to learn from failure. He sat down on the log, made

137

a shaky wire-crossing, and at the jump he went through a routine of static gymnastics, working himself up to the effort.

No. 11 on the other hand, the passive man of the written tests, plodded round the course with no distinction but no glaring faults, and showed a kind of stolid practical sense which was reassuring.

I also saw a new character to note—No. 7—a short, weak-faced little fellow with receding hair and an anxious manner. He refused at the jump.

After a while I walked back to the house and looked up No. 23 and No. 7 in the written tests. The Sergeant Tester, who, remember, marked the papers blind, having never seen any of the candidates, had written of No. 23: 'A soap-box orator. Over-emphatic, probably covering a deep sense of inferiority.' This seemed to me accurate to the verge of the uncanny and I questioned the Sergeant. He glanced at No. 23's papers to refresh his memory and pointed to responses which were printed in capitals, underlined and ran to sloganesque phrases such as 'Resist—to the last man.' 'Home—is my castle.' 'Mother—of all freedom-loving peoples.'

'Anybody who can take time to print and underline in fifteen seconds . . .' said the Sergeant darkly.

The timid No. 7 had written as his word-association for 'Illnesses and ailments'—'Indigestion'.

'A man who writes down minor things like that is apt to be over-careful and rather sorry for himself,' said the omniscient Sergeant.

Other word-reactions of No. 7 confirmed previous impressions. Against 'Resist' he had written 'war-time temptations'.

'Guilt?' pondered the Sergeant.

Many of his responses suggested anything but belligerency. 'Butt' had not suggested a rifle to him, but 'goat'.

138

For an association with 'Destroy' he jotted down 'rats', which might or might not be taken to cover the enemy. 'Death' produced the mild whimsicality 'Where is thy sting?' But his mildest of all was for 'Invasion'. He wrote: 'No bathing. Barbed wire.'

All through the day the psychiatrist was calling men up for interviews and the Colonel was interviewing steadily too, though on less scientific lines. He simply wanted to get an angle on each man to relate to the test results and opinions would be placed before him at the final consultation of the Board, over which he would preside.

I next went to see a squad tackle the Practical Group Test. Here the picture painted by the testing officer was that the men were faced with a raging river, represented by a leafy gully. They had to get across with a field gun, but the torrent was too fierce for any crossing in or on the water. There were some logs and ropes lying about and it was obviously a bridging job.

The minute the instructions were over a Sergeant wearing an Indian service medal (indicating a regular soldier of some years' service) snapped out orders and had everybody scurrying for a moment to his bidding. The testing officer let this outburst of highly vocal leadership go on for a moment and then asked quietly what he was doing.

'Lashing the logs together to make a raft,' said the Sergeant briskly.

The testing officer reminded him that it had been stressed that the current was too strong for a water-crossing. The Sergeant looked sulky, but the leadership passed out of his hands in a second. I looked up his psychological test report later. The Sergeant Tester had written simply but damningly 'Dullard—no problem.'

No. 7 was passive as ever. I noticed him standing well back, watching the bridging proceeding with an expressionless face. Most of the men had their coats off by now, but

139

No. 7 remained fully dressed. I asked the testing officer what he was supposed to be doing.

'No idea,' said the officer, looking puzzled. 'I'll ask him.' He strolled over, stood for a minute beside the little man and then spoke to him. It turned out that another candidate in a burst of inspiration had decided that the operation ought to be covered by a sentry, so he posted No. 7, who accepted the rôle of immobility without demur. He was returned to active duty at once but I never saw him do more than hold the end of a rope and look vaguely perplexed. I had the feeling he wouldn't break his heart if he didn't become an officer.

No. 11, on the other hand, had found something practical to do and felt more at home. He had climbed out on a log and was lashing it to a handy tree when the testing officer lit a firecracker in the bushes and when it exploded announced that an enemy shell had fallen, killing No. 11 and another of the more active members of the party. They had to drop out. The idea was to see how the party would react to the sudden loss of two of their leaders. No. 11 dropped down into the gully and out of the test, but he slipped and pulled down with him the log he had been sitting on. He landed face down in the leaf-strewn 'riverbed' and the log crashed on his head. He came up looking dazed, but he grinned, shook himself like a retriever and announced he was all right. It seemed to me the best mark he had earned all day.

Back in the Mess for tea, the Colonel told me he estimated that about half of this lot would pass. He had had one trying interview during the afternoon with a man in his thirties who had written on his personal history form, under the heading Father's Occupation, 'Country gentleman'. This character seemed to have bluffed his way through life, largely on an assured manner and a 'cultured' accent. I was professionally ashamed to find that his principal bluff had been to hold a minor magazine editorship for several years.

One of the features of the Selection Board system was that it eliminated any chance of a man getting through on class, or snobbish, grounds. There was a time when the passport label 'officer type' might be tied too easily on a well-bred nonentity who spoke well, played games, had gone to a 'good' school, and raised a well-trained moustache. The son of a country gentleman provided proof that the net was now too fine for such errors. He did badly in all the tests and his bluff did not impress the Colonel, who, at tea, was still chuckling over the fact that this candidate had thrown hopefully into the conversation the information that his grandfather had been a general.

In the evening I found the testing officers grouped round a chart which the candidates were never allowed to see. Down one side were the candidates' numbers. Along the top were headings for the various tests and also columns headed 'Tactical Sense', 'Guts', 'Control', 'Leadership'. Each little square below had a hole for a pin. Slowly and judicially the officers chose coloured pins from little bowls on the table under the chart and fitted them into the holes. Light blue meant 'very good'. Green was 'adequate'. Red meant 'bad'. Black was 'special case'. I watched the chart fill up. A man with a row of blues and greens was obviously in the clear. A man with a sprinkling of reds was in trouble. In one or two cases there was a disconcerting mixture of the more extreme colours, probably finishing up with a black. Looking along the column heads in such a case I could form some sort of picture of a man with good education, an ability to formulate and utter his thoughts, but no practical ingenuity and absolutely no resolution or dash that would inspire men to follow him. He might make an officer in an administrative job, but he was for the moment a 'special case'.

His fate would be decided at tomorrow's final board meeting, when everybody who had seen him at work or examined the result would contribute an opinion.

One of the psychiatrists had made a practice of talking to rejected candidates. He found there was little resentment or sense of grievance. The tests tended to make a man feel he had been fairly tried, had had a square deal, and that his failure was his own fault. Another psychiatrist told me that one of his colleagues went to a course for company commanders and interviewed the officers before they started. He compiled an order-of-merit list which was locked up. At the end of the five weeks' course it was compared with the Commanding Officer's list, drawn from the results of thirty-five days' solid work. They were ninety-five per cent in agreement.

The psychiatrist in question was present when this story was told. He grinned at me and said, 'Of course, you realise that in the other five per cent of cases the CO had slipped up.'

II

NO CLOAK, NO DAGGER

It was the strangest cocktail party I ever attended. Eight men and one woman—the hostess, a divorcée, whom I shall call Gertrude. I have no idea if she gave other parties for the same purpose, but anyhow it would be as well to cloak her identity. She was—and is—a very good friend of mine. In those days, early 1943, she ran a club in the West End of London and Anthony Cotterell (with whom I was still working) and I formed the habit of dropping in about 6.30 when he had finished our largely chairborne day of Army duty.

But this evening we had been asked to her flat, near Berkeley Square. What made the party strange, apart from its smallness and the disproportion of the sexes, was that all but one of the guests were men we were accustomed to meet casually most evenings in Gertrude's club. All but one. He was a tall, grey, tight-lipped, rather gaunt man and he grated on me. He had a quiet voice but a very intense manner of speaking. Everything, even the most casual over-a-drink small talk, seemed to matter terribly to him. He was constantly asking one's opinion and then challenging or bitterly opposing it. I moved away from him several times, but somehow I soon found myself in conversation with him again.

Then we had a row—not a scene, but a short, sharp flareup. An actress was mentioned whom I had known for at least ten years. I had no strong feelings about her either professionally or personally. I had always known she was

143

part-Indian. The merits of her performance in some film were being discussed by three or four of us when suddenly the grey civilian—who had been arguing that she had little talent and even questioning her beauty, which I would have thought unassailable—said, 'Damned *chi-chi*.'

The exact words that followed are not important; they were not many and our voices were not raised. I said I thought he had made as idiotic a remark as I had ever heard, as well as being offensive. He professed surprise, then when he realised I was not contradicting him about the woman's origins, but already knew, he was contemptuous about my naïveté; the attitude was, why not face it—she's *chi-chi*; it's true so why not say so? His grey eyes were steadily, intently, on me.

I left soon afterwards, still raging inwardly, though, I hope, not apparently. Those verbal rubber stamps, like *chi-chi*, are infallible in their power to infuriate me. I was going out to dinner with Cotterell and on the way downstairs he said, 'Well, what was all that in aid of?'

We were puzzled. It had been a perfectly innocuous cocktail interlude, but for my brush with the stranger, which was momentary and caused no embarrassment, but we could find no *raison d'être* for the occasion.

I remarked that everybody present had been old friends but for that grisly character who talked about *chi-chi*. Then we forgot the whole thing.

Next day my telephone rang. 'My name is Butt,' said a quietly harsh, urgent voice. 'We met last night at Gertrude's. Will you have lunch with me?'

I hedged. But soon I realised that, whatever the reason, he was prepared to suggest one day after another until I agreed.

We lunched the following Saturday, at Gertrude's club. In the interval I wondered why he wanted to meet again. During the first course he said, 'I want what I'm going to

144

say to be completely confidential. Agreed?' I agreed. 'I work for Intelligence,' he said. 'Would you like to do that sort of work?' At that moment I could think of nothing I wanted to do less, if it meant working with him.

'But I'm in the Army,' I said feebly.

He brushed that aside as presenting no problem. The first thing to establish was whether I was interested; he wasn't making me a firm offer but if I was interested he would arrange a meeting. . . . At least it sounded as though I wouldn't necessarily work with him, which was an improvement.

'Is this entirely your idea?' I asked. 'And did you just suddenly think of it the other night?'

He smiled. There was a cynical, almost bitter twist to his smile, but it was by far the most pleasant expression I had yet seen on his face.

'Oh, the other night,' he said, dismissively. 'Don't worry about that. I just wanted to see how you reacted.'

'You mean you didn't mean . . .'

'I didn't mean a thing. I wanted to see how quickly you got angry, if you lost control . . .'

'Did I?'

'Of course not.' He chuckled. 'I did needle you, didn't I?'

'But why? How do I come into the picture at all?'

'Oh,' he said airily, 'somebody mentioned you. We checked up. You seemed all right.' He rattled off a few facts about me, all accurate.

'So you wanted to have a look at me?'

'That's right. I looked around for somebody you knew that I knew. Gertrude. She has a rough idea of the sort of thing I'm in. I just asked her to arrange for me to meet you.'

At least that curious little party was explained.

'But what qualifications could I possibly have? A

145

journalist turned temporary soldier. I don't speak any languages.'

Inevitably when Intelligence is mentioned one thinks of spying in a foreign country.

'I know,' he said. 'Not much by way of education either —left school before sixteen and only been out of the country on holidays and short trips as a reporter.' He grinned again; it was becoming less forbidding each time. 'But I mustn't tease you again. They say Scottish education is very good.'

He outlined the sort of work his department was engaged in, but concentrated on what I—if I joined—would be first called upon to do. At last the solitary qualification appeared; I had experience as an interviewer and, he presumed, I could convey on paper the essence of an interview in a way that would be useful to the people who wanted the subject interviewed but didn't want to appear in person. It was rather a come-down from that momentary vision of glamorous espionage to realise that the first assignment would be interrogation based on a given brief, but I don't think any normal, inquisitive person in my position at that time could have done other than accept the proposition.

We had had two cocktails before lunch and Butt had insisted on a bottle of wine; now he suggested a brandy to toast our agreement. As I declined a thought struck me. 'I don't suppose it was accidental that your having a look at me took place at a cocktail party,' I said.

He smiled. 'It's as well to know about that sort of thing . . . you know what I mean.'

I assured him that if I had had the brandy I wouldn't have keeled over or burst into 'Auld Lang Syne'.

'You can never tell about security,' he said. 'But I'd guess yours is okay. You talk a lot but you can keep things to yourself. Right?'

I excused myself and went downstairs to the lavatory. When I came back I said, 'Talking about security, you

146

realise that under each of these tables there is a grill and if you stand under it downstairs you can hear everything that's said.'

He had a quick look and then gave me his most cynical smile. 'I don't think the enemy would have learned much,' he said.' 'But I think you'll do.'

Nothing happened for two weeks. I was particularly busy in my job and there were moments when I almost wondered if the whole Butt episode had ever really happened. One afternoon I was doing some research in an underground department in Whitehall—a vast place with scores of officers and ATS secretaries—when the telephone rang on the desk of the man I was consulting.

'It's for you,' he said.

I realised that I had not told anybody where I was going, and this was a place I had never visited before. Nobody knew me. I took the telephone. The harsh, urgent voice was unmistakable.

'Can you be at [he named a West End address] in ten minutes? Take a taxi. Ask for Colonel Blank.'

I still don't know how he traced me, but it was probably simpler than it seemed. I arrived at the place he had named and was immediately shown up into a large, handsomely furnished room with half-a-dozen men in it. I'm quite sure, looking back on it, they were not putting on an act but the effect was dramatic. Behind the large desk was a strikingly handsome, silver-haired man in uniform, rank of Brigadier. Behind his shoulder stood a saturnine civilian. (I decided he was the head of the Secret Service, using the Brigadier as front man, but when I came to know him later he turned out to be an amiable underling, concerned with administration, who just happened to look saturnine.) The other four men, mixed civilian and military, were scattered about the room. One sat on a window ledge looking out into the street most of the time and never spoke. My chair was placed uncomfortably about two yards away from the desk, in the middle of the room. I felt at once isolated and surrounded. There was no sign of Butt and it was weeks before I saw him again.

The Brigadier took me through the information about myself that Butt had quoted, so this time I was not surprised. He was friendly and easy and soon we were talking—very British this—about people we mutually knew. All the others except the man on the window ledge put in a question now and again, but it was all very relaxed and as far from the cloak-and-dagger atmosphere of such things in fiction as it is possible to imagine.

There remained only one last hurdle to be cleared, but it was not put to me like that, nor indeed at that interview at all. One of the men present telephoned me a couple of days later and asked me to come and see him. I found he was completing the arrangements for my transfer to 'special employment'. It was all set, he said, but it was the custom, and a very nice one he thought, for a new boy to be taken to lunch by what we shall call the Boss. Perhaps I looked apprehensive for he laughed and said, 'Don't worry. I'll tell you exactly what'll happen,' and he outlined a programme which began at 12.50 p.m. precisely, at a West End club, and concluded with a handshake on the pavement outside at 2.20 p.m.

When the time came I wished my new friend hadn't given me this deadly forecast, for as the programme was played out I developed a ridiculous inclination to giggle at its inexorability; to excuse myself, I should say that what was so risible was the thought of what would happen if I played the wrong card and upset the timetable. Exactly as predicted I was led into the bar, given a pink gin (I was asked what I wanted but somehow it was predestinedly a pink gin), asked if I wanted another (but he started to get to his feet as he made the offer); the bar clock stood at one o'clock precisely. In the dining room I was told they had a very good cold table and was led firmly towards it. We had coffee in the

148

hall; I was asked if I would like a glass of port but somehow the answer had to be No, thank you. And as he shook my hand on the pavement outside and turned away it was exactly 2.20. The work of the department of which my host was in charge had not been mentioned once.

As this particular Boss retired as soon as the war was over—he had been nearing retirement when it began—there is no harm in describing him. He was a big, heavily-built, slow-moving man; when he sat, he was absolutely still. He had kindly eyes and I never saw their expression change except to quiet amusement. In or out of uniform you would have said 'soldier' the moment you saw him. He was not inspiring but he emanated reliability; rock-like is the word for him.

He did not speak more than was necessary and he used plain words in short, unequivocal sentences; without affectation he had a totally decisive, judicial delivery, emphasised by a strong trace of Scots accent. He was a good listener, almost too good, for he let you talk until you finished or petered out. When he spoke there was a sense of this being a considered judgment and the last word on the subject, yet this was misleading, for he was not dogmatic and if you wanted to reopen the subject he was ready to let you.

In spite of his rigidly timetabled lunches, he normally gave the impression of being entirely at your disposal for as long as you wanted. I never heard him say anything that was not fair, practical and wise. I saw him many times over the next two or three years and admired him increasingly. To say he was imperturbable would be an understatement; no matter what fantastic, dramatic story you told him, no matter how seemingly insoluble the problem, he merely looked as though he had heard it all before and experience had put him beyond surprise or despair; as often as not he would suggest what could be done and refer you to one of his lieutenants to work out the details.

149

When only a few people knew the date and plan for D-Day he made one of his few general utterances. He warned us of two dangers—the danger, in certain circumstances, of saying nothing, and the danger of saying something which would reveal by implication what should be concealed. In other words, if somebody in your company said, 'I'll tell you what's going to happen—strictly between ourselves. We're going into Northern France on June 1' (the original date for D-Day), the temptation to button your lips was to be resisted. What would a man who knew nothing say naturally? Probably something like 'I say, really? June 1? Of course I'll keep it absolutely to myself.' Then you should find out if the man really knew, in which case he was in trouble. The last thing to do was to say, 'Ssshhh—you mustn't talk about it,' thereby confirming what might be just a know-all's lucky guess.

But D-Day was still a long way off, and I was soon in the midst of my apprentice job of interrogation. Much of this was routine and negative, but it had its moments. I once had to hold a man in conversation for a couple of hours, taking him tediously through the same facts while Special Branch entered his flat, found the evidence they needed, and telephoned me to release him. He was an unpleasant, cocky individual and when I let him go he seemed smugly satisfied that he had yielded nothing to a rather floundering and re- petitive junior officer. I escorted him to the street door of the building for the simple pleasure of seeing two men approach him, touch him on the arm, and lead him away to a long absence from public life.

Often the question I had to resolve was whether or not the interviewee should be 'landed' in the country. This may sound odd as he was already sitting across a desk from me in central London. But the position was that when people arrived at a port during the war Immigration and Field Security decided whether to give them permission to land or not. The Security man had not much time to make his decision, so if he had doubts he granted provisional permission, and passed on a message that they should be further interrogated. Some reported for their interview arrogant and impatient. After all they had been through (usually a journey from neutral Portugal after having stayed there as long as the authorities would permit) why should they be subjected to interrogation by a junior officer? It was often necessary to use some simple techniques on them. Some could be made more co-operative by irritating them, some by frightening, some by polite flattery. Some were cunning, some almost incredibly stupid.

An over-made-up, voluble matron sailed into my room one day, half-an-hour late for a noon appointment, announcing that this was all a ridiculous piece of red-tape and that she must leave in fifteen minutes for a luncheon appointment. She answered every question unsatisfactorily and made a number of uninvited speeches, mainly about how awful everything in Britain was. I deliberately kept her, bobbing on her chair, till 1.30 and then as she rose I said, 'Why did you alter your passport?' The passport had been taken from her at the docks; she might have guessed that it had come to me, though I had not produced it. But foolishly she decided to bluff it out and loudly denied ever having tampered with it. I opened the door for her and said, 'I want you back here at 2.30.'

I came back myself at 2.35 and found her waiting. She had been thinking, and I don't imagine she had enjoyed her lunch very much. I now produced her passport, but neither mentioned it nor opened it. Her eyes fixed on it and she was silent for a while. Then it all came out, simply and rather pathetically. She had had an affair with a Portuguese officer and when the time came when she was told to leave Lisbon her lover offered to see what he could do on her behalf. He asked for her passport. But she knew she was several years his senior, so she could not bear that he should see her date of birth. Not uncleverly—but not cleverly enough—she had made the alteration.

There was no evil in her, but in wartime you can't have even stupid ageing ladies arriving in the country with altered passports and refusing to co-operate with the authorities. She gave me a list of the people she had associated with in Lisbon and although one or two of them were, in fact, working for the enemy I'm sure she didn't know it and would have been no use to them anyhow. When I told her she could go—and that she should get herself a new passport—she was in tears of gratitude, unrecognisable as the woman I had met a few hours earlier.

Another eventually innocuous case was the lady I privately called Hedy Lamarr, whom she resembled and indeed matched for beauty. She was French but with a British passport, for she had—but had long since mislaid—a Gibraltarian husband. We struggled along in a mixture of French and English until I remarked that I was surprised that she had not learned more English in view of the number of visits she had paid here before the war. She raised her beautiful eyebrows and asked what I meant. I produced her passport and pointed out the stamps showing entry and departure from the country at least a dozen times between 1935 and the beginning of the war. Sometimes she had been in the country for six months at a time.

She denied the evidence of her passport, which baffled me. I said helpfully that perhaps she had many friends in England and had forgotten how often she had visited them. No, she said, even more bafflingly, she had no friends in England. It was deadlock and the more I questioned her the more her scanty English diminished. At last I called in a bilingual colleague. He had a gruff, clipped English voice and by biting out colloquial words in staccato asides he could give me a running commentary on their conversation, which I couldn't follow at all.

'Stone-walling,' he would bark out of the side of his mouth. 'Won't budge.' Then later: 'Tart, I'd say.'

He had hit it. A quick call to the Criminal Records Office and I found that the termination of all her visits closely followed on a London police court conviction for soliciting. But to the end she pretended ignorance. She, too, had made useful friends in Lisbon and had profited materially by them; her elegance was such as was never seen in Piccadilly or Shepherd Market before the Street Offences Act. She eventually swept out of my room, leaving a delicious wake of perfume, waving her jewelled hands and protesting that there had been some horrible mistake.

Of all the exotic and dubious birds of passage who alighted—and stayed as long as they could—on the Lisbon perch, the one who intrigued me most was one I never met. She was a French girl in her early twenties and, according to first-hand reports, dazzlingly beautiful and with great charm. She arrived in Lisbon with a wealthy protector who soon afterwards died, leaving her unprovided for. But she did not have to reduce her way of living, or do anything so squalid as go to work. Her social circle of international acquaintance was so wide, and she was so sought after as a companion, that everybody engaged in espionage in Lisbon took it for granted she was working for the opposition. Thus if she dined and danced with X, known to be working for the Germans, she would be approached by Y, an informant of the Allies, and paid to tell him what the German had asked her and what she had told him. X would then come back with an offer for her confidences on her evenings spent with Y. It was a long time before it was established that she had, in fact, worked for nobody, but simply enjoyed herself.

Mixed with the returning prodigals were what can only be called the maddies. In the matter of wild reports and the

153

private hallucinations of the spy-crazy (of whom there are an astonishing number) I was the end of the road. President Truman hung over his desk a notice 'The buck stops here'; there was nowhere I could pass those bucks that were so skilfully passed to me. If a man or woman walked in at the front door of the War Office, demanded to see 'Intelligence' and was interviewed either by an officer of one of the purely military branches or by the long-suffering civilians retained for the purpose of dealing with enquiries, the chances were that sooner or later he or she would wind up across the desk from me.

The commonest root of the more lunatic stories was persecution mania. 'They' (the amorphous enemy) were after them (the story-tellers). It was no good saying, 'Why should they be? What do they want with you?' You would usually get a crafty look, even a conspiratorial smile. Wasn't it obvious? One woman was convinced that the tenants of a flat opposite hers were photographing her. With a tele-photo lens? Oh, no, they got into the house while she was out and concealed tiny cameras about the place. What were the photographs for? They wanted to know everything she did. Did she do anything that would interest the enemy? The look told me I was being obtuse and unsympathetic and there was no point in her confiding further in me.

Most of them were confident that all their letters were being opened. Could I see some of the letters? Oh, no, they were private. I must have been told a score of times of 'absolute proof' that neighbours were operating a secret radio and kept sending morse messages in the night. The proof never materialised. Police checks always showed the neighbours as innocent as babes.

There was, of course, work other than on this lunatic fringe. But often even serious, sensible Intelligence operations have overtones of comedy or simple dottiness. Every now and then I had to call on a man who was retained for an

154

excellent reason: he had studied—indeed, I believe, practised—astrology in Germany in close association with the
man who was now known to be Hitler's astrologer. As
Hitler took astrology seriously, it was clearly advisable to
be kept informed of what he was being told. Our astrologer
lived in a West End block of flats and he was paid in cash
by hand of one of us. To keep him happy, we had to spend
an hour or so with him listening to what the stars foretold
about everything.

A colleague of mine who was normally concerned with
physical security, like the safe despatch of the Prime
Minister to meet the American President or Stalin, was
roped in one day for this chore. He was a rugged-looking
man with extraordinary, spatulate, gnarled hands, obviously
very strong. The next time our astrologer was visited he
said to the officer in great alarm, 'That man you sent last
time—what have I done wrong?—his hands—he is a killer.'
The officer, rather bored with all this mid-European hysteria, said, 'Oh, yes, we call him The Strangler.'

The astrologer never forgot. Whenever I called he
opened the door an inch or two and said 'Thank God—I'm
always terrified they'll send The Strangler again.'

Such informants were useful in their various specialised
ways, but they usually had their peculiarities. One of them
longed above all else to be an officer in the British Army.
Money didn't interest him compared with the glittering
prize of His Majesty's commission. He pestered the Colonel
in charge of this operation to the point of extreme exaspera-
tion. To shut him up the Colonel said one day, 'I've
arranged it. You're a captain in the British Army. Of course
I can't give you anything in writing. It's much too secret
and, of course, you mustn't use the rank.'

He was overjoyed, and gladly promised total secrecy.
But unknown to any of us he went out and bought himself a
uniform. He was an ungainly, fat man, foreign-looking to

155

the point of caricature, and the day I saw him walking down Piccadilly in service dress, looking like an unmade bed, I was torn between laughter and concern. He was quickly warned off the uniform (he was absurdly impressed that our spies had seen him the first day he wore it), but I am certain he dressed up from time to time and after the war I saw him referred to in a newspaper by his fictional rank.

As time went by I did less and less interrogating and became involved in other things more directly concerned—it seemed to me—with waging war. But occasionally, and flatteringly, I was called in to deal with off-beat cases. One day I was asked to interview an Englishman who had escaped from St Denis prison, in Paris. That was all I knew in advance. He was a thin, gentle, sad-eyed man with a brown beard and a slight stammer. He wore an ill-fitting tweed suit and he might have been an artist. We talked for a few minutes in a preliminary way and then I asked where he had been when the war began. He named a place in Northern France. I asked him how long he had been there. Fifteen years, he said. What was he doing there?

'I am a Trappist monk,' he said.

It is a sentence few people can have heard uttered.

The outline of his story was simple if extraordinary. He had served in the 1914–18 War and afterwards became a Trappist, eventually settling in this French monastery. For fifteen years he had observed the silence rule, with the normal feast-day exceptions. His British nationality was discovered by the Germans when they invaded and he was put in prison. He decided that for the term of his imprisonment and until his return to a monastery he could consider himself dispensed from his vows.

His escape, too, was essentially simple. He discovered that prisoners who became lousy were taken from the prison to a hospital once a week for baths and treatment. He deliberately infested himself with lice. For a time he went

156

quietly to and from the hospital in a van with one German guard. He kept his eyes open for an opportunity to escape. One winter afternoon the van was returning to St Denis in the dusk when it ran into a cordon across the road. A bomb had been thrown and the Germans had sealed off the area while they sought the culprit. The German guard got down to see what the hold-up was. The Trappist got down too and walked away, without haste, into the dusk.

After that his story was the routine one of that period—the slow, hazardous journey south, finding his way from one patriot who would help to the next. He had been caught on the way, imprisoned again and spent months scrubbing floors. But again he patiently awaited his opportunity and escaped, eventually crossing the Pyrenees into Spain.

At the end of our interview I asked him what he was going to do now. He looked mildly surprised, and said he was going into a Trappist monastery in England in a few days. I asked him how he thought he would like returning to the monastic life after his long and adventurous excursion into the world of men and speech. He looked at me with a gentle smile and said quietly, 'It'll be a nice change.'

12

I WAS MONTY'S DOUBLE
ONCE REMOVED

ONE AFTERNOON in March 1944 my Colonel buzzed for me
twice. Both buzzes were memorable. He was a heavily-
built, restless man who usually peferred to wear civilian
clothes (which our curious Intelligence status permitted)
and, with cigarette ash permanently sprinkled down his
rumpled blue suit, he cut a distinctly unmilitary figure. This,
while natural to him, also served his purpose; he was, in
fact, a regular soldier, but, although he had spent more of
his adult years in uniform than out of it, 'soldier' was as unlikely a label as you would ever have hung on him by guesswork.

When I answered the first buzz, the Colonel was pacing
up and down his room and he bustled me over to a wall map
which showed the south coast of England and the north
coast of France. With a remarkable economy of words and
gestures, and therefore, the maximum drama, he put me—
as the phrase was—'in the picture' about the plan for the invasion of Europe, then timed for June 1.

I was still thinking over the implications of this dramatic
news when I was summoned again by the buzzer. This time,
before I was properly in the room, he barked, 'Who could
impersonate Montgomery?' I was fairly new to working
with this colonel—let us call him Colonel Logan, as did the
film which was eventually made of this episode—but I felt I
knew him fairly well. His bark was a mannerism; unless

158

you had done something very stupid (or somebody high up had and you were catching the backwash) there was no bite. He had a strong dramatic sense and he liked to shoot startling questions, to which quick answers were required. He was a stimulating if sometimes exasperating man to work for.

'Miles Mander,' I said.

'How tall is he?'

'If he stood up straight he would be close on six feet, but he stoops.'

'Too tall. Anyhow, he's in Hollywood, isn't he? Who else?'

'Look,' I said, 'I can't produce two Montys out of a hat. Let me think about it.'

'Right,' said the Colonel, 'see you in the morning.'

I have a goodish but erratic memory and during the rest of that day something nagged at the back of my mind, as if I had somewhere an answer to this problem, if only I could dredge it up. I lay awake that night trying to search systematically for some clue or association, then, typically, the answer came all in one piece. It was a photographic memory. I had seen a newspaper page with a picture of a man in a beret. I remembered taking for granted that it was General Montgomery until I read the caption. Then I found that it was a photograph of a man who had walked on to the stage at a troop show to take his bow as producer, had been cheered by the audience as Monty, and then revealed himself as—but what he revealed himself as I could not recall.

In the morning I telephoned the Colonel and told him I was working on the problem and would not be coming into the office. Not very confidently I thought it was the *News Chronicle* in which I had seen the picture, but after an hour or two turning the pages of the files I almost decided I was wrong. Then, suddenly, I came on it. It was just as I had remembered and the man was named as Lieutenant Clifton

James. Back at my office I went through the Army List, but there was no officer identifiable as Clifton James. The number of Jameses made me quail, but I started sending for their personal files in batches. For the next day or two I was invisible behind a rampart of files on and around my desk. Again I was tempted to give up, but persevered. Exactly half way through the alphabet in terms of Christian name initials I was rewarded. There was a Meyrick Clifton James serving with the Royal Army Pay Corps, who seemed about the right age and who was an actor in civilian life. He was stationed at Leicester. It was time to make a progress report to the Colonel.

'Trustworthy?' that insatiable man barked when I had finished my story.

'How should I know?' I said; 'and anyhow, what's it all about?'

All I knew at this point was that somebody was required to impersonate Monty; the Colonel filled in the whys and hows for me. Somebody—to this day I do not know who—had had the idea that while the cross-channel invasion was being mounted General Montgomery should ostensibly appear in another theatre of war.

It was becoming increasingly impossible by then to conceal the assembly of men and materials in the South of England. Enemy reconnaissance must have shown that something was in preparation and the irresistible conclusion was a cross-channel attack into France. Assuming that knowledge, the enemy must be asking two vital questions—when and where? If General Montgomery, who was bound to be one of the leaders of an Allied invasion, was reported to Berlin to be in the Mediterranean the enemy would draw one conclusion and might be tempted by one speculation. The conclusion would be that the invasion of north-west Europe was unlikely to be imminent while Monty was out of England; the speculation would be that another attack was planned—across the Mediterranean from North Africa into the South of France. Some strength would be given to the speculation by the fact that signs of preparation had no doubt been reported from North Africa, for, although on nothing like the scale of the English Channel attack, there was then being mounted in North Africa the attack which went into the South of France about two months after D-Day.

Thus our assignment was to find or create a figure sufficiently like Monty to be mistaken for him, and to exhibit the dummy (while, of course, seeming to conceal him as we would if he *had* been General Montgomery) in places where the news of his presence would be reported back to Berlin and, at the very least, cause some doubt, uncertainty, and desirable confusion as to the Allies' intentions and what should be done to counter them.

Already, although we had no 'Monty', the Colonel had decided where he ought to go. A brief call at Gibraltar and then an arrival at Allied Forces Headquarters in Algiers would, he thought, be at once logical for the Commander of our notional operation and would be likely to yield to the enemy the necessary leakage of his presence. But, although D-Day was still nearly six weeks off and our deception should be executed as close to D-Day as possible, it was urgent that we find our double and make our plans. The first step was to have a look at Clifton James, but without his realising why he was being looked at.

'I'll go up to Leicester,' said the Colonel suddenly. 'Think up some pretext.'

This was a favourite trick of Colonel Logan's. Instead of saying 'How can we have a look at James?' he was proposing something which was impracticable and, on the face of it, even foolish. He could not go unannounced and snoop around the Army Pay Office in Leicester to have a look at one junior officer; and looking would not be enough— we would have to find out what sort of man he was. It was

161

up to me to fill the gap and make the Colonel's trip to Leicester a viable proposition.

In cases like this, a kind of elementary, brain-cudgelling logic is the only hope. Why would a senior officer from London want to interview James and not through the proper channels of his Commanding Officer? Who in the War Office would be interested in James? He was an actor. Who was interested in actors? ENSA? Army films? This kind of unbrilliant thinking sometimes produces a momentum which will make the mind jump several steps ahead to the answer. Suddenly I had it. In the Directorate of the Army Kinematograph Service David Niven was a lieutenant-colonel. In his position it seemed reasonable enough that he might want to borrow a professional actor for a part in a film. Niven had the great advantage in my eyes of being a friend who knew where I worked; his well-known name could cut two ways. It might open doors or it might create resistance. It all depended on the people in charge at Leicester. It was certainly a good enough idea to act on.

It could be said that the Monty's Double operation went into gear in the casual encounter of two officers on a corner of St James's Street one lunch-time. What David did not know was that, remembering he lunched as often as not at Boodle's, I had lain in wait for him. What I hoped to promote was best done as informally as possible. I simply told him I wanted to make contact with an officer serving in Leicester and perhaps David might act as the lever by which the man could be prised loose from his unit without too many questions being asked. He gave me a long, steady look with his bright blue eyes and then responded as ideally as though I had written the line for him. 'But, of course, old boy,' he said. 'Ring me in the afternoon and give me the details.'

The next episode is, of course, not within my personal experience but the Colonel and James described it to me

162

later. An excited ATS telephone operator rang through to James in the Leicester Pay Office and gasped, 'Oh, sir, it's London calling. You'll never guess who it is.' On that level, the film star name produced its effect. As an ex-regular soldier, David Niven knew quite well what the 'channels' ought to have been, but he played it much more cleverly by his seeming ignorance of procedure. He simply told James that his name had come up as a possible for a part in an Army film, but that, as it was all very much in the air, he did not want to approach his CO formally at this stage. However, a colleague, a Colonel Logan, happened to be passing through Leicester next day and would James meet him for lunch and a talk? David Niven had never seen James, so he had no inkling of our purpose; but we had created a perfectly good excuse for Logan and James to come together without any need to confide in anybody.

The Colonel came back satisfied that James was, super-ficially at least, our man. Another telephone call from Colonel Niven to Leicester and James reported at Curzon Street House. What more natural than that after a few minutes the busy Colonel Niven should retire and leave James with his colleague, Logan? Some more talk, and James was handed a printed form. It was the relevant extract from the Official Secrets Act. James was told to read it carefully and then sign a declaration that it had been brought to his notice.

When the Colonel came back to our office it was my turn to have a spasm of canniness.

'You're sure he's all right—he won't leak?' I asked.

'I think so,' said the Colonel, then he grinned. 'Anyhow,' he added, 'it wouldn't be the end of the world if he did.'

'How?'

'Because I told him the story in reverse.'

One is always especially impressed by the twist one failed to think of one's self. Logan had told James he was to

163

impersonate Montgomery *in the UK* while Montgomery went to the Mediterranean to launch the invasion. Suppose, at the very worst, that all James knew reached the enemy. A Mediterranean invasion was precisely the idea we wanted to sell them.

After that I saw a lot of James. While the rest of the plans were being made there was nothing for him to do but hang about. Not unnaturally, it made him restive and nervous. We did not want him seen coming and going at our office, which made it worse. I used to meet him in the mornings on a street corner and we would drink coffee in the Kardomah in Piccadilly and talk. When I had other work to do, I would pack him off to the pictures. I wouldn't like to think how many newsreels he saw in that period.

Fortunately, James was a pleasant companion and while I could do nothing to allay his nervousness by giving him the information he badly wanted about exactly what he was going to have to do I could keep him reasonably cheerful and advise him on security to cover his being in London. I came to know him well and this was reassuring because there was no doubt about his intelligence, his willingness to do what was required, and his common-sense about secrecy.

Even his nervousness was all right; what I had dreaded was an over-confident know-all who would take the thing too lightly, whose vanity would endanger security (and after all he had, as an actor, landed a plum part), and who would collapse when the time came.

Through this period, as we made our careful arrangements, letting as few people as possible into the story, I was constantly bombarded with questions about James from Colonel Logan. One day he demanded, 'Can he fly?' This hadn't occurred to me. It would be too bad if our Monty arrived at Gibraltar green-faced and rubber-legged from air-sickness. But how to establish his airworthiness if our story to him was that the impersonation was to be done in the UK? Between us, the Colonel and I worked it out that we could tell James that among his Monty duties would be to show himself in Northern Ireland, inspecting troops or something. We added colour by saying that leakage from there via Dublin was likely. I asked the question and James told me he had never been in an aeroplane in his life. With the help of a pilot who was employed on secret missions we had James make a flight to Devon and back. It was made in a tiny two-seater plane in bad weather and James emerged successfully.

At last the deadline drew near and we had a full scenario worked out. To let James have a close study of Montgomery we transformed him into an Intelligence Corps sergeant and attached him to the General's bodyguard, first on a South Coast tour and then on the fishing holiday Montgomery took in Scotland when he had everything set for D-Day.

James had a miserable time. He was not strong physically and he had to sleep in damp tents and ride in open jeeps in bad weather. Several times he was reprimanded by officers and for failing to salute or say 'sir'. He had served in two wars, but never before in the ranks.

He came back from Scotland exhausted but with a new spirit in him. He had met Montgomery, very privately, and he was now right inside the part. He had caught the distinctive carriage and expressions; he could mimic the voice excellently (though it wasn't strictly necessary), and he had picked up several mannerisms. It was when he was showing me exactly how Monty saluted that I realised something we had overlooked. James had a finger missing from his right hand. It seemed terribly conspicuous when he saluted. This snag was overcome by ingenious bandaging so that the 'General' merely looked as if he had had a slight accident.

Without any help, James made himself up—extra grey at the temples and on the moustache—so that with the double-badged beret the likeness was uncanny. At his two

165

ports of call only the Commander-in-Chief and one other officer would be in the picture. James learned names, studied photographs, and memorised some 'in character' conversational gambits.

We held rehearsals. Chairs represented the aircraft and, although we were all very serious at the time, it must have been a funny sight, with one of my colleagues, the late Marcus Haywood, representing the Governor of Gibraltar (though we couldn't use the name as James didn't know where he was going) and Colonel Logan, in civilian clothes, as the guard of honour, presenting arms with an umbrella while 'Monty' inspected him.

We had fitted James out by this time, which was easy enough, except for the medal ribbons. For these we had to get General Montgomery himself to put in an order with his own tailor. At the latest possible moment we told James that the plan had been switched and that he was going to the Mediterranean. I think that if we had told him he was to drop by parachute into enemy territory it could not have added to his anxieties; there is a point beyond which more worry is impossible. This did-not bother me, and fortunately the Colonel too knew something about theatre people. Actors can be like jelly in the last days before a new play and rock-like the moment they step on stage. Again, I would have been worried if he had been less than petrified.

The departure was to be at night, so that evening we held a dress rehearsal in my office. The Colonel's secretary was there as a kind of wardrobe mistress, checking the clothes to be worn and those to be packed. Suddenly I realised that a tropical shirt lacked the badges of rank—and we had no spares. The Colonel blew up, justifiably, I suppose. It was too late to get Montgomery's tailor. Then the secretary, a quiet, pretty girl, spoke up. 'I believe I can help,' she said.

'How?' Logan barked. 'What d'you mean you can help?'

'Well,' she said, very diffidently, 'Daddy's a general.'
The Colonel looked as though he were going to kiss her. Instead he patted her and bustled her off to rob Daddy's wardrobe, and that problem was solved.

It had been decided that James should be accompanied by two officers—an ADC and a senior staff officer, rank of Brigadier. Here I fell disappointingly between two stools. I didn't look young enough and smooth enough to pose as an ADC and at the age of thirty-three I could not claim to look like a plausible Brigadier. Nor could I argue the casting of these two rôles. We borrowed a young man from the real Monty's entourage and he looked just right (he was, however, very airsick and had to be practically carried off the plane at Gibraltar, so as a performer he was virtually a nonstarter). For the Brigadier, my colleague, Marcus Haywood, was chosen. He was perfect. A major like me, he was in his fifties. He had been a regular soldier in his youth. He was handsome, silver-haired, and moustached, not too old, not too young, and had a quiet air of senior authority to which I could not aspire. Marcus got the job, and I have seen many Brigadiers not nearly so well cast for the rank. But I had taken it for granted that as I had been closest to James from the time I 'found' him I would follow through at his side. I felt (if James will forgive the simile) like a puppet master who has to stand aside at the last moment and let somebody else manipulate the show.

I have always thought there was something characteristically British—or do I mean English?—about the period immediately before the great departure. We drove out to Marcus's sister's flat in Kensington, James in a plain cap and trenchcoat. While James changed and made up, Marcus's sister, a gentle, distinguished-looking woman in late middle-age, served whisky and soda and sandwiches. How much she knew I cannot say, but she treated us as though we were simply friends of Marcus who had dropped in for a drink,

167

and when James emerged from a bedroom in full rig as General Montgomery she did not bat an eye, but merely offered him a drink and a plate of sandwiches.

This was James's last drink for a while—for as Monty he would be a non-smoking teetotaller—and with it he had his last cigarette. He tackled both ravenously. He then covered himself up in his trenchcoat and we started out for Northolt. A little way short of the airport he slipped into his beret and out of his coat. At that moment, he told me, he felt at his lowest. He was sure his make-up was wrong, his beret askew, and that nobody would ever take him for anything but a ludicrously bad imitation of the real thing. Then, as the car halted in traffic, some people by the roadside stared in and began to wave and cheer. James looked aghast, but recovered quickly and waved back. It was *our* best moment to date, for in that one moment James became Monty; the face and wave were exactly right. He was an actor and he was 'on'. I knew we were all right.

A big York was lined up on the tarmac in the fading light. A dozen or so high-ranking officers stood around. There was a moment of absurd, amused satisfaction (especially when they all came to the salute) in the realisation that of those present only Logan—raising his battered homburg and looking, I suppose, like 'somebody from Whitehall'—and I knew that we were seeing off a lieutenant in the Pay Corps.

The Colonel went off and briefed the crew. Their captain, a much decorated wing-commander who had experience of VIP flights, took the news expressionlessly, thought for a moment, and then said, 'The only thing to do, sir, is to treat him as though he *were* General Montgomery —every moment of the way.'

The operation went according to plan. This part is almost anti-climactic. (When, years later, the idea of filming the story was broached to me I pointed out that it lacked dramatic shape; it was a long, detailed build-up to a brief, virtually uneventful climax and sudden fade-out. I was wrong, but you can see what I meant.) The staging at Gibraltar and Algiers was discreetly done. That is, ostensible efforts were made to keep Monty from the public gaze, as would have been done if it had been the real general, yet care was taken that suitable people should have the opportunity to learn of his presence and yet think they had penetrated a secret. By lunchtime the following day James, having breakfasted with the Governor of Gibraltar, walked in at the front door of AFHQ, Algiers, as Monty and emerged by a back door a few hours later as a moustacheless lieutenant in the Pay Corps.

It is typical of Intelligence operations—and I am criticising nobody and nothing except human nature—that our meticulous planning petered out almost immediately after this moment. Obviously James had to lie low, and we had asked that a place might be laid on in which he could do so. But if the Colonel thought farther than this he never told me, and I certainly didn't. The one officer in Algiers, apart from the Commander-in-Chief, who was in our confidence arranged that James should stay in a villa whose normal occupant, a senior officer, was away.

Haywood delivered James there and encouraged him to relax, which he was only too happy to do. But Marcus, whose acquaintance was world-wide and high-level (I shall never forget the day I consulted him on a problem involving a trip abroad by King George VI and he picked up the telephone, said 'Get me Buckingham Palace' and fixed the whole thing on an old-boy basis) had met some old friends in the HQ Mess who insisted that he dine with them. All James wanted was a quiet evening and early to bed, so Marcus had no compunction about leaving him. There was a resident soldier-servant in the house and James was told to ring for anything he wanted.

169

After a while James decided to arrange for his dinner and rang the bell. It was dusk and he barely looked at the man who answered. The servant fetched James a drink, took his instructions and then just stood. James looked at him. The soldier was obviously going through some mental convulsion. James too felt something stir in his memory. They stared at one another for a moment and then the servant said incredulously, 'Jimmy . . . the Desert Song . . . Derby . . . 1928.' I cannot vouch for the show, the town, or the date, but neither can James and it was something like that. Anyhow they had been together in a touring company of a musical years before.

Fade-out, fade-in . . . when Marcus Haywood arrived back late that night the first thing he saw was a chink of light showing from the otherwise blacked-out villa. He dashed in, could find no trace of James, and drawn by a curious sound —if it wasn't 'Sweet Adeline' it was 'Nellie Dean'—he penetrated the kitchen quarters. There at the kitchen table were James and his old stage chum nicely merry after a splendid dinner, reminiscing about the good old days.

Obviously James, even as himself and without his moustache, should not be seen in Algiers at the same time as rumours of Monty's presence were (we hoped) going round, so next day he was sent off by air to Cairo. He did not know when D-Day was, so he had no idea how long his incarceration might go on. But he was comfortably housed in the flat of an Intelligence man and he continued to relax. Then one day he was flown home, and, of course, without proper documentation, he had a much less easy time than on his journey out. However, one morning he telephoned me to say he was back in London and we met. He was understandably thrilled that all had gone well, and more especially that it was all over. We were delighted with him and without making promises, which were too dangerous, I undertook, with the Colonel's backing, to do everything possible to secure some reward for his services which could fairly be described as above and beyond the line of duty.

James went off to his Pay Office desk in Leicester and we did try to have him rewarded in some way. We started by trying to get an OBE for him, but it was too difficult because at that time we could not fully explain what he had done. We tried to get him promotion but ran into the insurmountable obstacle that a captain in the Pay Corps had to have some particular accountancy qualifications and James—the poor actor!—couldn't meet such requirements. But at last we did something, probably of more practical—not to say artistic—value than anything we had thought of before. For every day that James had impersonated Montgomery, from the time he took on the rôle until he came home, we somehow managed to get a reluctantly grateful government to pay him the full rate of a general.

There may remain in the reader's mind one important question about the operation: did it really work? The evidence is that it did, or at least that it was a factor in events that ensued. The Germans had a substantial force, including armour, in the South of France and when the going was tough at Caen and Falaise we watched the Intelligence maps avidly. The Germans were slow to move their forces north, though it was—or might have been—greatly to their advantage to do so. There was a hesitance which we felt sure meant that they had not made up their minds about the threat from the south, and Monty's reported presence in that theatre undoubtedly reinforced the threat.

Later still, several captured German generals told their interrogators that they had heard of Montgomery's 'secret' arrival in the Mediterranean. One said he never doubted it was a feint—but he never doubted either that it was Montgomery. This interested me greatly because during the operation, at some moment of difficulty, I had said that the right way to work this deception was to use Montgomery himself. There was time enough, of which Monty's fishing holiday in Scotland was in itself proof; characteristically, he was ready to the button-pushing stage well in advance. But I'm afraid I was scowled at, and I cannot blame anybody. To fly one of the most important commanders of the greatest invasion of modern times to another theatre of operations and back, at a time when the skies were by no means under Allied control, would have been a risk I doubt if even a Churchill would have been prepared to take.

I went on leave soon after VE day and the day I came back my Colonel buzzed for me once more. He tossed a wad of typescript towards me and said, 'Have a glance over that. James has written his story and submitted it for approval. We can't release it yet of course but let me know what you think.'

I had always enjoyed playing detectives with Colonel Logan, who was far better at it than I, which was in itself a challenge. An hour or so later I went back to his room and said, 'The story's all right and we can lock it up until it can be released, but how many people now know all about it— and can we trust *them*?'

The Colonel looked at me fiercely. 'What people?'

'Well,' I said, enjoying myself thoroughly, 'there's the man who wrote this, and the person who typed it . . . and where's the original?'

The Colonel seized the typescript. It was a very clean, clear carbon copy, but patently a carbon copy; he had overlooked that. Where *was* the original? In whose hands? Then, as I pointed out, James had a finger missing, and the typewriting was so good and even that it had evidently been typed by an expert with all eight fingers operating—a touch typist. As for the writing, it was riddled with clichés and what can only be described by that old-fashioned word 'journalese'.

Two Special Branch men went to Leicester that night and,

I am afraid, gave James a fright he did not entirely deserve. He had, in fact, sworn to secrecy a close friend who was a journalist in private life, and the same man had done the typing. The carbon copy had been sent to us in error and the original was safely locked up by James.

It all worked out quite happily. The following year James was allowed to release an approved version of the story to a Sunday newspaper, and he therefore made some welcome money. Since then he has written an autobiography, the main feature of which is the Monty's Double episode, and the story has been filmed, with James playing himself with great skill and distinction. (He proved himself, in fact, a better actor than any of us had guessed.) He soon became popular as a lecturer, talking of his experiences as Monty's Double, and despite ill-health he kept up these performances—and the public kept asking for them—for many years.

My wife met James a number of times in post-war years when, with the passage of time, he had come to look even more like Monty than he did at the time of the impersonation. One night in a restaurant we were told by the proprietor that Monty had reserved a table. When he came in my wife—who had never seen Monty before—said, 'It can't be—he isn't nearly enough like Clifton James.' Time had changed Monty too, and she was right.

13

APRIL IN PARIS

IN THESE days of the four-minute warning of impending annihilation things must be geared to move very fast in military organisations; but all things considered, and in spite of the not unearned reputation of government departments for paper-shuffling and avoiding decisive action by the use of high-stacked pending trays, some things happened in the distant days of 1939–45 with remarkable speed. Lord Alanbrooke, who knows better than I, might not agree, but it seemed to people around my level that this was Churchillian in origin. The celebrated 'Action this day' technique must surely have had its chain-reaction downwards.

Whatever the cause, it was not only possible but a frequent occurrence, in 1944–45, for matters which had been before the Joint Chiefs of Staff at their morning meeting to reach by early afternoon a committee of which I was a member, representing a section of Intelligence. From field-marshal level to mine (I was a major) in a few hours, via at least two intermediate levels, was good going.

This happened one day in April 1945. The committee elected me to execute the task called for and before the Joint Chiefs could have had their afternoon tea their (to them) unknown emissary was making arrangements to fly to France.

The Army Council had complained to the Joint Chiefs that certain newspaper reports were suspiciously akin in content and phraseology to a Top Secret document to which they had given minimum circulation, and they felt there had been a leakage which ought to be traced. There was a Top Secret file on the subject and as there was no time to have the documents copied I had to take it with me. Unfortunately, I had it in my hand when I went to tell the administrative head of my department why I was going to be absent for a while. He noticed the red-stamped classification on the cover and as I was leaving the room he said, 'Have you got a bag?' After six years I was still civilian enough to think he meant a suitcase. But what he produced from a cupboard was a canvas sack about half the size of a coal bag. It seemed a ridiculous container for one foolscap file, but he dived into the cupboard again and to my horror came up with an ingot of lead, all of twenty inches long and about three inches thick. He put this in the bottom of the sack and handed it to me.

The idea, of course, was that if my plane came down the Top Secrets would sink and so avoid falling into enemy hands. As the enemy was now being battered into surrender in Germany and, I would have thought, in no mood to bother much about leakages in English newspapers, the whole procedure struck me as ludicrous, apart from the inconvenience it caused me. The very weight of my small handgrip with this sack at the bottom was suspicious in itself.

Otherwise I was delighted to be making a trip to Supreme Headquarters at Rheims and Paris. There was nothing dangerous nor even dramatic about going to France some ten months after D-Day, but as I had flown out of France in the last days of peace there was a certain personal significance about flying back in what were recognisably the last days of the war in Europe.

Next morning I reported to a house in a West End square. The white-cap on the porch tilted his chair back down on to its four legs and said: 'Hold the line a minute, honey,' into

175

the telephone propped on his chest. He covered the microphone with his hand.

'Yes, sir?' he said, polite but languid. 'Can I help you?'

It was a beautiful morning and the quiet square was shot with sunshine through spring leaves. It was so peaceful that the sight of an American military policeman seemed incongruous.

It was strange not to require a passport for a trip abroad. I did not even need a ticket; instead of cashing a cheque into francs I had been given a roll of spending money and instructions how to draw more on the other side. Instead of dragging myself and my luggage to a terminal to join a 'bus for the airport I was to be chauffeur-driven to the very flank of the aircraft. On the other hand, I had to equip myself with a Movement Order, a mauve-smudged sheet in quadruplicate, unimpressive but all-powerful in its effect.

As I collected it from another languid American private that morning, in what had been the drawing room of the house, I read it carefully. Once military wheels are set in motion they are difficult to brake or reverse and a GI's slip might have landed me, protesting but unavailing, in Rangoon instead of Rheims. However the few typewritten lines were accurate enough, though it had never occurred to me till then that my return to the Continent would be at the terse command of an unknown American colonel, ordering me to 'proceed to Rheims, France, thence to Paris, France' and in due course to 'return to proper station'.

I was the first of the three passengers to check in at the airfield and I was chatting with the Security Control sergeant, who was collecting pessimistic data about my next-of-kin, when the pilot bounced in. He was a plump, smiling young extravert in RAF uniform. Without introductions, he included me in his smile and chatter from the start. Engagingly he darted from subject to subject, using the firmly established argot of the airmen. Every male he men-

176

tioned was a 'type'; when he criticised someone for stupidity, that was a 'clueless type'. Even 'wizard'—that schoolboy adjective of enthusiasm which I had always thought became RAF usage in about 1940 only because so many of its users were fresh from the classroom—came out with unashamed frequency.

'Where's Mac, the old basket?' he demanded of the Sergeant. 'That dim type owes me three hundred francs. Still over there? Hope he doesn't come back before tonight. I could use those francs. Not that three hundred gets you far, but it helps.'

He turned and thrust a fountain pen towards me. 'How much would you say that's worth?' New fountain pens were practically unobtainable in England at the time so I said I would be glad to give five pounds for it.

'Would you?' he said eagerly. 'I gave four hundred hard-earned francs to some Frog for it. I thought he was *marché noir* and I was being gypped.'

I began to regret my high offer, as I had a perfectly good pre-war pen, but there was no danger. He had already put it back in his pocket, forgotten.

'Been to SHAEF Forward before?' he asked. 'Wizard snack bar they've got. Open twenty-four hours a day. All kinds of fruit juices. Great bloody glass of orange juice for ten francs. Mmmmmm. Wizard for the old hangover. Going to Paris? Lucky man—if you've got a bed. No-where to lay your head. It's no vice to go to the brothels. Bloody necessity. If I can get a lift I'll be there tonight. Never miss it. Wizard bloody place, old Paree.'

The two other passengers arrived and the pilot vanished. I saw him again for a moment on the airfield at Rheims and when he saluted as our car drove off I took a moment to recognise him. In his flying clothes he wore a completely serious expression and seemed ten years older, a different man.

177

The geometrically neat fields of France looked miraculously unscathed until I began to notice occasional clusters of silver medallions, shining in the sun. It was hard to realise they were bomb craters full of water. At Rheims the first words I saw were German—'Rauchen Verboten' in three-feet high letters on the gaunt wall of a burned-out hangar. Some GIs were silently and gracefully throwing a ball from hand to leather-mitted hand by the ruin. As we drove to the town the gable-painted advertisements for Dubonnet and Byrrh, faded and scaling, greeted the 1939 memory like friends who have suffered and aged but are bravely surviving.

A round-faced young soldier was in charge of the billeting office. 'Let's see,' he said, 'you'll have room 13 at the Hotel Monopole, sir.' I felt he was still savouring the subtle pleasure of giving orders to officers, but he did it civilly. I thanked him and asked where the Monopole was. 'Place d'Erlon,' he said, which was not much help to a stranger. 'It's the main drag,' he added. 'You can't miss it.'

The Monopole was a small, dingy hotel and only the pungency of floor wax countered the impression that it had been abandoned by humanity. The clumping of my boots on the bare stair stirred nobody but at last I found a scribbled notice, in English, on the wall, announcing that arrivals should report to 'the Madame' on the first floor.

There were five doors and three of them were locked. In the fourth room an American major was taking his boots off. In the fifth, half-a-dozen women and children and one man were eating their evening meal and a wave of warm garlic air passed between their questioning faces and mine. The man was a GI, so I addressed him. Later I found that each of these requisitioned hotels had a resident Army clerk who was responsible for liaison between the billeting authorities and the 'Mesdames' who ran the places. Strictly, the soldier should have taken charge of me, unlocked my room, and

178

generally acted as receptionist. In fact, he remained seated and chewing, and informed me that room 13 was on the third floor. Madame unlocked it and from that point service ceased, except for the making of the bed.

Room 13 was no grimmer than any other cheap provincial French hotel room, but that was quite grim enough. The cotton sheet was pale grey and somebody had written 'Sonia' over and over again, boldly and vertically between the floral tramlines of the wallpaper. I had a pound of coffee beans in a paper bag for a friend in Paris and on the journey the bag had burst. My bag had been borrowed from a friend and when I shook the coffee out on to a towel on the bed a small metal hair grip and two hairpins fell out. I was about to throw them away when I remembered that such things were scarce in England and I put them in my battle-dress pocket. That such feminine trivia could have an important effect on my immediate future I could not then guess.

I had been told that for eating I could choose between the Hotel Lion d'Or (American) or the Hotel Crystal (British). Going back up the street, or main drag, I came first to the Lion d'Or and went in looking for a drink. There was a small bar at the back and I ordered a dry Martini. The bar was busy and as I glanced round I noted the high incidence of red tabs on the collars of the British Army officers present. There was only one major apart from me and he was with a general.

I looked around the Americans. Nothing but eagles and stars. I tried the RAF. No wearer of the thin sleeve-rings had fewer than four and most sleeves had the thick ring of air-commodore. I was musing that it was natural to find many high-rankers at Supreme Headquarters when the truth suddenly came to me. I was in the senior officers' Mess for full colonels and above.

They behaved admirably. Nobody gave me a critical look. The barman had made no class-conscious distinctions

179

about serving me. I finished my drink and left. It did not seem the best start to make in a new place. The trouble was that nobody had told me that the hotel part of the Lion d'Or was so reserved and that it was in the restaurant I should put my thirty francs on the desk and eat my excellent dinner of US rations, French-cooked.

My first meal eaten in France since 1939 was not quite what I had dreamt about. The food was good, but there were incidental difficulties. A French girl clip-clopping over the floor in her elaborate wooden shoes, her hair piled high, tried to pour coffee into the large cup by my plate before I had properly started my soup. Short of causing a nasty spilling accident I could not stop her. When I had eaten in American Messes in England the waitress had always hesitated over this coffee-during-food rite, presumably because of my British uniform. It was only necessary to murmur 'later'. But now I was in the hands of waitresses who recognised no difference between one Allied uniform and another. For the first time in my life I had a large cup of coffee by my side as I ate *rosbif.* I consoled myself with the reflection that it might have been hot chocolate, which was also going around.

It was still daylight when I finished dinner, so I wandered around the lovely old town. The cathedral, disfigured by a high wall of sandbags all laid the wrong way round, with the seams to the outside, bulked reassuringly in the dying light. I finished up in a café—a humble, friendly *zinc*—where local champagne, running from thin taps, cost about a shilling a glass. I fell in with a Canadian-Jewish corporal and an Australian airman. The Canadian was in an amiable mood, having lately been seconded from less attractive duties to deal with prisoners of war who claimed to be his fellow countrymen. He provided the final sieve to check their purely Canadian bona fides, a safeguarding measure against infiltrators with a good tale. The Australian engaged on the same task was less happy. His dark blue AAF uniform was practically unknown to American soldiers in Europe and completely mysterious to the French. He had on several occasions been addressed in German and asked strange questions by persons who had misread his shoulder-title and thought he was Austrian. But the incident which worried him most was when a casual acquaintance asked him if they had got the Japs out of New Zealand yet. It took several stanzas of conversation before he realised that the stranger was confusing his country with New Guinea.

I began my detective work early next morning. I carried a letter of introduction to an American colonel of Intelligence (I also carried a 'to-whom-it-may concern' document from the Chiefs of Staff, requiring that I should be given every facility, but to my chagrin I never had occasion to use it), so I walked the short distance to his office in a champagne company's requisitioned building. It was a warm morning and the colonel sat in a small office with the windows shut and the central heating full on. He read my letter and then asked me to put him in the picture. I was in battledress, which is not indoor spring wear, and half way through my recital of the situation my head began to swim and I had to ask for a window to be opened. Then I could not remember how far I had got with the story. It did not matter, as it turned out, because he was a slow-witted man and I think he was grateful to hear the facts twice.

I suspected he was not going to be much help in sleuthing, for as I talked he interjected low whistles and 'Geez' and 'You don't say?' I was accustomed to more sophistication in Intelligence officers. However, he directed me to a useful man on Eisenhower's immediate staff and by noon I had established enough facts to know that my next enquiries should be made at the rear echelon of Supreme Headquarters in Paris. I asked about transport, which was unexpectedly difficult, but at last I found a transportation officer who promised that if a car was going to Paris that day at all I should be given a place in it.

I went off to have a quick lunch, undertaking to be back by two o'clock sharp. At twenty minutes to two I finished packing in room 13 and turned to open the door. There was no handle. It was one of those locks consisting of a series of metal layers and after I had damaged my nails and numbed my fingers I decided it was impossible to fight my way out of the room with my bare hands.

It was now a quarter to two. I opened the window which looked over a courtyard. There was neither sight nor sound of life. I yelled 'Madame'. There was no response except for the echo off the buildings on the far side. I yelled again, and again. The thick peace of siesta hung over the place. In the midst of these despairing yells I noticed something on a widow ledge at right angles to where I stood. It was a white porcelain door knob. I leaned out and eventually reached a delicate point where my thighs were across my own window ledge and my finger tips were on the other ledge. Slowly, painfully, I inched forward, my trunk now wholly suspended three floors above the yard. Gradually I closed my fingers round the knob, which tended to slither away as I touched it. At last I was able to grip it and began to worm my way back. It was ten minutes to two. I could still make it.

But the handle did not fit. Perhaps all the door knobs in the Hotel Monopole are planted in unexpected places to give an extra spice to the life of the transient. I do not know. But my hard-won knob and my bedroom door had obviously never met before, nor were they at all closely related.

I cursed myself for having given up carrying a jack knife (with bottle opener) which I always did before I was commissioned. I scratched ineffectually some more, and then I remembered the hair grip in my pocket. Ask me for a piece of stout wire at any normal time and I shall fail you. The odds against my having such an item on my person are high, but when combined with the chance of the need for such a thing arising they must be astronomical. The bent wire slid the lock back easily. A little out of breath, I reached the garage at exactly two o'clock and had to wait for an hour before the car left for Paris. I made good use of the time, however, for I put my Top Secret file at the bottom of my bag and 'lost' the sack and ingot behind some convenient packing cases.

My companions in the C and R (communications and reconnaissance) car to Paris were a British woman officer who had had measles and was going to have a week's convalescent leave at a Paris YWCA (which, by the way, was what Rumpelmayer's in the Faubourg St Honoré had sunk to) and a hard-bitten GI driver who had never made the journey before. This alarmed me but, after a little preliminary confusion caused by the scarcity of functioning bridges out of Rheims, he neither made a false move nor asked a question from there to the Madeleine.

The sharpest nostalgic sensation I had experienced since the gable-ads at Rheims came with the first scent of Paris on the hot dusty air of a premature summer evening. I decided it was compounded of perfume, French cigarettes, and horse manure (though all three were in short supply) and it was intoxicating. Another sensory characteristic of Paris at that time had been added by war shortages. It was aural. Almost all the women were wearing shoes with wedge-soles of wood, leather being unobtainable, and the men wore metal toe and heel tips to give their shoes longer life. The result was a combination of clip-clop (feminine) and click-clack (masculine) which for the first twenty-four hours was deafening and inescapable and thereafter, by one of those adjusting processes in which nature is so kind, inaudible.

The thick-necked driver dropped me off in the elegant courtyard of the Rothschild house in the Faubourg St

183

Honoré which was now the British Officers' Club. Our warlike vehicle and dusty battledress probably gave a wholly false impression that we were straight from the battlefields. I saw no reason to regret this, as the officers of the British Staff, strolling in for their aperitifs, looked far too highly polished.

Not wanting to overdo the soldier-from-the-war-returning act in case I met somebody who knew I was currently spending most of the time chairborne in London, I repaired my appearance and had a couple of low-priced (but also low-powered) drinks in the club and then walked up to the Hotel Chatham. I had asked one of my contacts in Rheims to telephone ahead for me, so I was allocated to share a magnificent room, with private bathroom, with a young and taciturn American lieutenant-colonel. I am sure he was virile enough, but from the number of times in that short period he told me that the arrangement was for one night only, that his room-mate was only away on a quick trip to London and would be back next day, one would have thought I had been thrust into the menage of honeymooners temporarily parted. I was not sorry to move out, as the colonel appeared to have two shirts which he wore alternately, the second hanging on a hook in the bathroom. It frankly stank, but he changed into it for dinner and back to the other (which was no fresher) in the morning.

I pursued my enquiries that evening with some amiable and hard-working officers of the censorship and made some progress. The pieces of my puzzle were coming together now in a predictable way and it seemed almost certain that the leakage was going to be traced to a stratospherically high level and would probably be complete just as the war ended, when nobody would care.

Before dinner a dapper little officer in British Intelligence Corps uniform reported to me. His name was Captain Beaufort. He had a French mother, a half-French father, a

184

French wife, and his home was in France. He was bilingual with only a slight accent. He had been assigned, he said, to assist me in every way possible. His foreignness made me toy with the idea that he might be an enemy agent, which would have been more fun, but I could not conceive why the enemy would be interested in my activities, so I decided to make use of him as guide and companion, but, as he offered no credentials of any sort and was vague about his normal duties, I did not confide in him. This, in Intelligence work, is known rather splendidly as the elimination of the elementary risk. I suppose one thing that put into my mind the wild notion that Beaufort might not be what he claimed was his over-stressed insistence on 'we' and 'our' when talking about the British. When he told me, for example, that one thing all foreigners admired greatly about 'us' was 'our organisation' I was confused for a moment, and asked what precisely he meant.

'Our rationing,' he said. 'They'll ask you which rations you actually get—a question which usually baffles an Englishman at first because there are no rations we don't get. That's what impresses them. You see the ordinary Frenchman with no pull often doesn't get his ration. The grocer gets it, but by the time he has taken care of his family and his relations and his "circle of reciprocity", which may include his doctor and his lawyer and the priest, there is likely to be nothing for the man who just presents his ration card.'

When we discussed the inflationary situation Beaufort quoted the aphorism that the *petit rentier* class had eaten their houses, thus summing up a little-publicised tragedy arising from the French love of retiring from work on a pittance at an earlier age than is common in other countries.

Answering several of my questions about what seemed anomalies of the Parisian scene, Beaufort was forced to shrug and murmur: '*C'est défendu, mais c'est toleré.*' He

185

hated speaking French with me, but I could see his difficulty when it came to such essentially Gallic phrases. When I remarked on the number of rather pasty-looking young men, usually flashily dressed, who seemed to spend their days hanging around the cafés, Beaufort read me a little lecture on *Système D*, an institution which was regrettably *toleré* and as unhealthy for the country as the young men who lived by it. The 'D' stood for '*débrouillé*', for which the best translation is probably 'smart'. Naturally, during the occupation the definition of this kind of smartness was extended to anything which put one over on the Germans. It is difficult to pull back the boundaries of definition and especially to persuade youngsters who learned to operate 'Système D' in their formative years that what was smart in the occupation was immoral and criminal now when the Germans had gone. A dozen times I had quoted at me the saying: 'For four years the black market was a patriotic duty', which, while stating a truth and a problem of transition, did not alter the fact that far too many young Frenchmen (and a lot of not so young ones) continued to live more comfortably than their fellows in a *débrouillé* world in which the acquisition of a few packets of American cigarettes and their disposal across or under the café table at ten times the price represented a day's contribution to the economy of *la patrie* under reconstruction.

A more legitimate use of the power of the cigarette-packet was demonstrated by Beaufort himself. In one Service club he took me to he was shown the most remarkable deference and given first-rate service by the French *maître d'hôtel* while far higher-ranking officers were having difficulty in getting tables. This priority was purchased for twenty cigarettes at discreetly spaced intervals.

Beaufort was the most unquestioning obeyer of orders I have ever met. Whatever I asked him to do he did at once. Sometimes when I found him too assiduous in attendance I simply told him to meet me at a certain place at a certain time and he would salute and vanish. (Did he click his heels or did I imagine it?)

One afternoon I had an appointment at Versailles and was assigned a jeep and driver for the trip. I dismissed Beaufort and went in search of my driver. He was waiting for me in the lobby—a bright-eyed, black-haired little fellow in GI uniform. I naturally assumed he was what he seemed to be, an American soldier. But his first word, as I got into the car, was '*Rapidement?*' uttered with a shining eagerness of inflection. The combination of a French driver and a jeep struck me as a formidable prospect, so I replied with a craven series of '*Nons*' and much head-shaking.

He told me his name was Maillot and his home was in Algiers. He spoke little English but was eager to learn. I asked him how he came to be in the American army and not in the French. He had been in the army of General Leclerc, he said, and had entered Paris with it. But he had been *blessé* on the way and was eventually discharged. He had three small sons and one of them was delicate. The climate of Algiers was not good for him, so Maillot *père* had decided to stay in Paris and work for the day when his wife and three boys could join him. But why, I asked, did he join the American army? He looked at me, his shoe-button eyes grave for once.

'To eat in Paris,' he said slowly in English, 'it is necessary to be in the American Army.'

Maillot was living well within his pay and saving for his family reunion. In a moment his eyes were sparkling again and he was speaking French vivaciously. He asked me if I would like to see his boys. We were nearing the Etoile and the traffic was thick. Maillot was, to say the least, an impatient and impetuous driver. Before I had answered he was unbuttoning his blouse pocket and rummaging in his note-case. He held the steering wheel with his elbows. I took the wallet from him and extracted a photograph of three

187

attractive, dark little boys. Any hope I had that Maillot would return his attention to the business of driving was not fulfilled. He leaned over me to look at the photograph and to tell me the boys' names.

But there was plenty of light relief from the hazards and tensions of the journey. Maillot decided he liked my 'English' accent and in the midst of one of my more laborious French sentences told me so, adding abruptly 'Speek Eenglesh'. Almost at once he entangled himself in the intricacies of the verb 'to go' and in the end I'm sure I left him with the impression that 'I 'ave went' was good popular usage.

The best moment of the trip came on the way back through Auteuil. A woman deep in thought passed slowly in front of us when Maillot had calculated that his announcements of his coming would accelerate her safely out of our path in time. He drew up sharply and the woman belatedly looked up and scowled. She must have assumed that here was a perfectly ordinary jeep with a perfectly ordinary American soldier driving it, and she let fly with a phrase or two of shrill Parisian comment. Maillot pursed his mouth in an expression of restraint, dropped both hands from the wheel in a gesture of despair, then raised them in front of him, palms upward, to shoulder level as if to bring an orchestra to its feet. Then he exploded.

'Madame,' he said, and so on.

The woman stood gaping. So did several other passersby. Amazement and admiration showed on their faces. An American with *that* command of down-to-earth French? Or some strange kind of impostor? They looked baffled and, in the end, beaten. Maillot dropped his voice suddenly and calmly resumed the conversation with me, in his struggling English, where he had left it before the incident.

It began to rain and Maillot became unsure of his way. He yelled at two passing priests. One of them, in moderate

188

English, gave us a direction and then added that he was not sure. Maillot demanded indignantly in French why, in effect, he should keep two busy soldiers hanging about in the rain giving them directions which were clearly unreliable and a waste of time. The priest apologised very humbly and Maillot graciously accepted the apology.

My work was nearly finished now; only some routine filling in of gaps remained. And rated as a detective story it was rather a poor one. At Versailles I had found a senior officer who had a copy of the Army Council document. It was mimeographed and numbered 118. As the Army Council had originally circulated twelve numbered copies and only two of these had gone to France, it was obvious that somebody, with or without authority to do so, had duplicated and circulated the paper on a multiple scale, thereby spreading to absurdity the field of possible sources of leakage.

I was satisfied that the Versailles officer had not shown the document to a newspaperman, but had quoted it with too great accuracy. The other leakage had not come from the same source, but with at least 118 copies floating around I had the choice of tracking them down individually, which would have taken weeks if it were possible at all, or settling for a report which pinned the blame on the man who had given the order for the duplication. I was in no hurry to leave Paris, so I decided to make a few more enquiries in the next couple of days and at the same time enjoy some stolen leisure.

In fact it all worked out even more swiftly. I was leaving the office of an American general one day when his attractive WAAC secretary called me into her room. She knew my mission and thought she might be able to help. She had gone to Rheims one day in the company of the second newspaperman involved, and when she went in search of him to start the journey back, found him in a very senior

189

officer's room reading a file. He asked her to wait while he finished it and on the journey back to Paris told her the gist of the story he later wrote; it was clear he had just gleaned the information from what he had been reading.

The organisation I worked for had an office in Paris at this time, but so far I had worked alone and had had no need of my colleagues. Now, however, I màde contact with them and went along to the luxurious flat near the Trocadero which they were occupying.

It was a bizarre set-up. In frilly, much-mirrored bed-rooms girls I had known as civilian secretaries in London were now in khaki, perched on beds and sofas with their typewriters on their knees. I was lucky in that a friend of mine—a senior officer whose counsel I respected second only to the Boss's—was over from London and I had an hour with him in a salon obviously planned for smart parties rather than Intelligence conferences. (The explanation of this setting had a certain irony. During the occupation the tenant of the flat had been a British agent whose speciality was playing the rôle of eager collaborator and entertaining Germans socially. The first action of his heartless employers on reaching Paris after the liberation had been to turn him out of the flat.)

My colleague listened to my story, approved my deduc-tions, and agreed that I should remain in Paris long enough to tie up the ends and make some notes to ensure that I did not find a link missing when I came to write my report in London. So the next few days were pleasantly leisurely. I delivered the coffee I had brought—and what was even more welcome, news of her relatives in London—to a friend in the suburbs. She was an elderly English woman, the widow of an Italian and long resident in Paris. Her daughter had been caught doing resistance work and shipped off to forced labour in Germany and the mother had to look after her baby grand-daughter. With food conditions as they had been, this was an anxiety and the child had a fragile beauty which enchanted and yet frightened me. (She died not long afterwards.)

They were living in a tenement and I hammered on the door for a long time before the old lady opened it an inch or two. Her relief on seeing me was pathetic; she had heard my heavy Army boots on the stairs and that, followed by thumping on the door, had terrified her; she could not get used to the idea that the Germans had gone.

I remembered one much more trivial mission I had promised to carry out. When I borrowed the bag in which I had found the hairgrips the owner asked me if I could bring her back some perfume. It was *Je Reviens* she used and I duly queued at Worth's one day for the hour or so when the shop would open and sell its small daily quota. When the queue moved up inside the shop I found myself beside a row of sample spray bottles. One was labelled *Je Reviens* and, realising I had forgotten what it smelled like, I idly picked it up intending to spray a little on my hand. But the spray was low and probably faulty and what happened was that a large, last gasp of perfume spewed out and soaked the cuff of my battledress. *Je Reviens* is a lingering scent and I had only one uniform with me. For the remainder of my stay at the Chatham I had to suffer some odd looks—and ribald remarks from my friends—every time I stood at the bar. Noses began to wrinkle as they wondered where the powerful and hardly masculine aroma was coming from.

I had dinner with a colleague who had just pulled off a successful coup and, as so often happens, it had been achieved by a mixture of the observant eye and pure chance. A British subject arrested and accused of helping the enemy had stoutly denied a charge that he had addressed meetings in Paris on behalf of the Germans. One day my friend was passing near the Crillon when he noticed a tattered scrap of a poster on a wall. An English name caught his eye and he ripped the fragment from the wall and put it in his pocket. Enough print remained on it to establish that it was an announcement of a meeting the Englishman in custody had addressed.

Transport was scarce and I made my way about Paris mainly by walking and using the Metro. The excitement of liberation had long since died down and there was an uneasiness to be felt in the streets, which were heavily sprinkled with rather aimless GIs on leave or off duty.

Surprisingly few American soldiers in Paris seemed to have troubled to learn more than a word or two of French and their faith in the power of American English, spoken loudly, as an international passport to communication appeared to be as firmly rooted in them as in a well-known type of travelling Englishman. In the Trocadero station of the Metro one day I came on a GI who was yelling despairingly at a newspaper seller. I intervened hopefully. The soldier shouted: 'Goddam them. They won't tell you a goddam thing. I've been saying "Ahpra, Ahpra, Ahpra" to that guy for ten minutes. Goddam it—"Ahpra"—it's the same in any language.' I decided the nuance would be too subtle to explain to an angry man, so I merely told him that if he came with me to the station I was going to he would be within sight of the Opera. And I said 'Opera'; it would probably only have complicated the issue further now to say 'Opéra'. He returned to his etymological convictions and to placate him I agreed that the word was the same in any goddam language.

In the Metro it was the evening rush-hour and my GI friend was jammed close together with three attractive French girls as we all clung to the same pole. He watched them intently, his face only a few inches from theirs, as they chattered. At length I saw he was speaking to them though I could not hear what he said for the noise of the train. They looked puzzled but gave him cautious smiles. At the next

192

stop they got out and he gazed after them. Then he turned to me and said sadly: 'So goddam pretty and not one of them speaks a goddam word of English.'

There is no doubt that many Parisians at that time were not kindly disposed towards the Americans. On the other hand those I met who recognised me as British were almost embarrassingly welcoming. This puzzled me and I asked a Frenchman to account for it.

'Oh, yes, the Americans are unpopular,' he said, which was no answer.

'And the British are popular?' I persisted.

'Oh, yes.'

'But why?'

'Because they are not here,' he replied with a sad smile.

I had run into an old newspaper friend, now an RAF Public Relations Officer, who had become an authority on the current Paris night life. I resisted his pressure to have a night out until my work was done.

Army life having impaired my stamina for late nights, I decided to concentrate my excursions into the world of the *boites* in one grand sortie the night before I left.

The evening began after dinner with something like a tactical conference at the apartment of M. Danton, a man who used to run a Paris night club but refused to do so again until things returned to that Utopian state he described wistfully as normal. My airman friend (whose name was Oliver) and I sat round the Danton dinner-table drinking the first pre-war quality *filtre* I had encountered and a wonderful liqueur which our host had nursed through the occupation. He told us many stories of the occupation, an eternally fascinating subject. One man he knew had pre-served his large cellar intact by a device which was based on the falsity of the legend of German 'thoroughness'. This man acquired one of those open-fronted shops in the vege-table market district. It was, like all such shops, littered with

rubbish and trade impedimenta—boxes, barrels, straw, bur-
lap bags, and cabbage leaves. He removed all this and little
by little moved his wine from his cellar at home to the cellar
of the shop. Then he restored all the litter. He gambled on
two facts: that nobody but himself knew the wine was
there and that German searchers of the premises would not
be thorough enough to move the jumble of litter to find the
trap door. It worked. He never went near the shop during
the occupation but when the Germans had gone he went
back and found the place untouched.

M. Danton's own escape, in the psychological sense,
during the long four years had been the study of a series of
trade guide books to the wine districts. He concentrated
especially on the Burgundy country. His guides, which he
showed us lovingly, gave a detailed map of every vineyard
with its vital statistics and history on the opposite page
Before the war he had thought himself a pretty good expert
on wines. Now he was vinously omniscient. He could
recite the output of scores of vineyards in the year 1938;
he knew more about the local and domestic vicissitudes of
little-known wine-growers than the average man knows
about his home town. But, more important, in these
esoteric studies he lost himself for whole evenings. He
achieved what every good Parisian desired; he completely
forgot about the Germans.

He had selected three night clubs for us. They could be
summarised as the dignified, the rough-and-tumble, and
the homely. The first was the Monsigneur, sombrely impressive with its heavily framed oil paintings and hazy red
lighting. There was no question of ordering. A champagne
bottle in an ice bucket was placed on the table and some four
pounds demanded. (This was the same in all three *boites*.)
The bandleader wore a white tie and his musicians would be
more aptly called an orchestra than a band. I counted fourteen violins. The cabaret consisted of two fully-clothed

female singers. The table on my left was occupied by a very ordinary-looking young couple, who worried me. They had ordered their third bottle of champagne before we left but they seemed quite sober. He bought her everything in sight; cigarettes, which were extremely scarce and dear; chocolates in a large ornate box; a huge bunch of long-stemmed, rather tired-looking roses. She did not seem particularly impressed. As he took a roll of notes out of his pocket to pay for each purchase I had the impression of a man eager to spend, as though there were a positive pleasure in the act of handing over the money. They looked more like a couple who ought to be saving up to get married. They made me uneasy.

For contrast M. Danton took us next to a honky-tonk. It had the comic overtones of caricature. The young woman who announced the cabaret wore a black suit, the coat of which reached below her hips. A thick curtain of blonde hair shut off half her face and reached to her collar bone. The hand in which she carried a foot-long cigarette holder was cocked back at the wrist, as if to burlesque an affectation. Next to me sat two young women holding hands tightly under the table. Near the band there was a table of half a dozen mixed American and Canadian officers, happily, a little noisily, but quite inoffensively drunk. Every time the band started one or two of them came over to the next table and asked the more feminine of the hand-claspers to dance. She refused with a curt movement of her head. But the men were not put off. At length one possessed of more charm and persuasion than the others talked himself into success and the girl, with a quick exchange of understanding smiles with her friend, rose to dance with him. At once another of the officers approached and asked the remaining girl to dance. She seemed surprised and annoyed at first, but the pink and smiling face of the officer, so obviously innocent, made her suddenly change her mind.

195

She smiled, shrugged, and got up. When I left she was dancing cheek to cheek with the pink face whose eyes were closed in ecstasy. She had a curious smile, amused yet slightly mocking, as if she deprecated this odd experiment yet was finding it quite enjoyable after all.

We drank our final bottle of champagne up near the Place Pigalle about four o'clock. Oliver was a little anxious by now, as he had to be out at Le Bourget early in the morning to catch a plane to London. This was the homely *boite*, bright and not full, where the stout, middle-aged owner sat and drank with us except for the occasional moments when he unexpectedly stepped up to where a quartet was playing and sang a chorus in a fruity tenor. The Madame who had been taking admissions had quit now and came and sat with us too. Over on the left, against the wall, there was a French party of two couples in the midst of one of those loud, uninhibited rows which cause no great public interest in Latin countries. The two women were screaming at each other across one of the men. The other man sat quietly opposite like an interested spectator. The little man across whom the battle was flowing leaned back taut on the sofa for a few minutes, then he banged the table with his fist and stood up, the decision to go written on his weak, angry face. Neither woman looked up, but one of them put her hand up to his stomach and pushed him back into his seat. This was repeated four or five times without variation.

A fan dancer came on, a slim woman of perhaps thirty-five with a serious, business-like face. As she circled the floor she passed close by a table where a pleasantly Allied group of NCOs—British, American, and Canadian—were drinking. A big British corporal had removed his blouse and was cooling off in shirt sleeves and highly-coloured braces. As the fan dancer came past she swept her fan embracingly over his head. Then she threw it to the orchestra leader and continued her circle of the floor. I watched the

196

corporal's face. He was entranced. He laid his large muscular hands on his wide-apart knees and sat up straight. 'Jesus George,' he said, slowly and loudly.

For no reason, except perhaps that the dancer's routine lacked the continuing stimulus of variety, I suddenly thought about the job I had come to France to do. A more inappropriate ambiance for settling an Intelligence problem would be hard to imagine. (Yet wouldn't a fiction writer on such a subject relish the incongruity?) It was clear to me how I should wind up my task. I would end my report with every clue and every point of evidence leading irresistibly to the VIP who had undoubtedly 'leaked'; then I would break off and add: 'I submit that further enquiries should be pursued by Supreme Headquarters within its own theatre of operations.' Nice windy stuff; discreet too.

Rather pleased with myself—the long steady intake of champagne is conducive to euphoria and self-satisfaction—I turned my attention back to the show.

The lean, business-like nude went by again and I watched as she passed close to the corporal. Again he vented all the joyful amazement of the innocent abroad.

'Jesus George,' he boomed. 'Jesus George.'

14

THIS WAY OUT

TOWARDS THE end of 1945, during which the British Army successfully concluded its operations against Germany and Japan, it was faced with a minor problem, indeed minescule at first glance but apparently presenting unimagined difficulties. It had to demobilise me.

My qualifications for release were impeccable, by age and length of service, and I was placed in Group 17, the official date for the demobilisation of which was October 8. But there were still snags. Four years earlier I had been posted from my regiment to be a junior staff officer. After a year I was 'lent' to Intelligence. I had resisted transfer to the Intelligence Corps, which would have involved exchanging my rifleman's black buttons for brass and the proud red bobble on my cap for the Intelligence Corps emblem, once unkindly described as a pansy resting on its laurels. Thus I was nobody's baby; not regimental, nor staff, nor orthodox 'I' officer.

Unaware of any complications I awaited the order of release and arranged for that essential preliminary to demobilisation, the 'medical'. I reported to that Thames-side architectural horror, Queen Alexandra's Military Hospital, known to most soldiers simply as 'Millbank', so that the Army could officially declare me fit, having given me the last chance to cite any complaints I might have or forever hold my peace, at least so far as pensionable ailments were concerned.

The MO was a young captain I guessed to be a Viennese

198

Jew. He was charming and capable, but he seemed a queer type to be playing such an important part in my exit from the British Army. His English was sufficient but quaint. When he tapped my naked back while I breathed through my mouth he said: 'You haff cold now, yes?' I said yes, I had a slight cold.

In flattering anticipation he wrote down as 'nil' the result of the urine test I had not yet had.

'Eef it is not you come back, yes?' he said. 'Many times we find the sugar. Eet is ver' important.'

I went through the ceremony of the lager glass in an outer room and an orderly confirmed the negative result and I was free, my certificate in my pocket.

October 8 came and went. Then I was told, because I pestered people to tell me something, that my date would be October 12. More pestering and I was told by different people that I should probably (a) have to go to my regimental holding battalion, now at Barnard Castle, county Durham (250 miles away); (b) that of course I would be demobilised in London like everybody else working in London; (c) that of course I could be demobilised in London as my home was in London; (d) that I should probably have to go to the Intelligence Corps depot at Rotherham, Yorkshire (164 miles).

This confusing information gradually fined down to Rotherham as a practical certainty. Then the London prediction hardened again. And on the afternoon of October 11 I was told I had been posted to the holding battalion at Barnard Castle, with effect from the next day.

I was old soldier enough to telephone the Adjutant of the battalion to say I was coming. If possible, and when there is no shooting war on, I like to know I have a bed. The Adjutant sounded alarmed. 'I don't really want you *tomorrow*, old boy,' he said. We eventually settled for Monday, October 15. But before we got that length there was a

199

moment when it was my turn to be alarmed. 'I'm not quite clear what you're coming up for,' said the harassed Adjutant. 'Oh yes, you're on an overseas draft, aren't you?'

I had a vision of myself being carried aboard a Far Eastbound troopship, screaming in vain that I was in Group 17.

It was bitterly cold in county Durham and the camp was indescribably bleak. The black metal stove in the barnlike Mess was inadequate. The inmates, amiable enough young men, sat around turning the pages of newspapers and periodicals.

I wandered into the Mess dining room for tea and sat with a group of officers I did not know but who greeted me with hospitable smiles and nods and went on with their conversation. Suddenly I was slapped on the shoulder and looked up to see a man I had known in my first battalion five years earlier. He was a Regular and I had liked and admired him; we had been on training exercises together and he had knowledge and experience and an enviable way with the men under our command. He had been a major then but apparently he had not made exactly spectacular progress, for he was now a lieutenant-colonel. He was, in fact, the Commanding Officer of the battalion which I had, at least nominally, joined.

'Hello,' he shouted, 'look who's here? Why, you old so-and-so. Haven't seen you for years. Where've you been? What on earth brings you here?'

The Mess was staring by now and it certainly gave me face to be greeted in such boisterously friendly terms by the CO. I thought his face fell when I said I had come to be demobilised; perhaps he was short of a company commander and hoped that a newly arrived major meant a replacement.

We reminisced about men who had been with us five

years ago, but I was woefully low in regimental news and gossip. I don't think he could quite grasp that I had been out of touch with the regiment solidly for more than four years. However, when he got up from the table he asked if I had been shown my quarters and when I said I hadn't he detailed a subaltern to look after me.

We walked across the wind-blasted heath to a hut and I was ushered into a cell-like room, furnished only with two small iron bedsteads with brown mattresses. On one of them sat a man a few years younger than myself, writing music on lined paper. Around him on the mattress books and notebooks were spread out. He looked up as though he resented the interruption, but he stood up politely, smiled and introduced himself. The subaltern vanished.

My room-mate and I exchanged a few sentences and then he said anxiously and apologetically, 'You don't mind if I get on with this, do you?' and resumed his notation. I found that he was preparing to be a candidate for the music-mastership of a public school when he was de-mobilised.

A batman arrived and asked me if I had any blankets and when I said I hadn't he said, 'Oh!' in a hopeless sort of way and stood surveying the bare mattress until I began to fear that that was going to be the extent of my bedding.

When I came in later, having had dinner and gone to the camp cinema in search of warmth rather than entertainment, he had found two scratchy blankets. He had not risen to a pillow, however, but with a bundle of clothes wrapped in a towel under my head and my British Warm on top I slept well enough. But nobody, except a boy straight from the cheerless discomfort of an English public school, could pretend to like this sort of living and I shall never sentimentalise about the dear old days in camp or Mess.

Next morning the sun was shining and the autumn fields and foliage of county Durham had a beauty which in the chilly dusk of the previous day was unimaginable. It was a pleasure to walk the mile or so from my quarters to the battalion Orderly Room where I was due to attend for the mystic purposes of 'documentation'. A sergeant, working at a cigarette-burned table amid that dusty litter which is peculiar to Army offices, writing with a Government pen in that fast neat hand which is the speciality of Orderly Room NCOs, contrasting incongruously with their work-manlike, square-topped fingers and usually broken nails, took me through the intricacies of the Release Book or Army Book X803. This was a masterpiece of the form-maker's art.

The idea was that I should fill this up and, in due course, take it to York (the area headquarters) and then to London, where a series of people would tear out the pages one by one for their various purposes. For the moment my day's work consisted of handing over my record of service and answering questions about my military past. This occupied from 10.45 to 11.10 a.m.

I wandered back to the Mess and wrote letters. On a grassy rise a hundred yards or so from where I sat at a window, a party of riflemen were training. An officer and a sergeant stood on the crest, inspecting and criticising the concealed positions the men had taken up. It was all 1939 re-enacted. There might have been nuances I could not detect at this distance but the outward signs were of the ageless Basic Infantry Training. No reverberation from Hiroshima had reached the Army in county Durham.

By lunchtime I had fallen in with another demobee-major, Matthews, a contemporary whom I had come across in London before he went parachuting in Italy and Greece. In the afternoon we decided to pass the time exploring the town of Barnard Castle. The Mess Sergeant, whom we consulted before leaving, said, 'There's a museum some-where around, but I don't quite know where.'

He couldn't have looked very hard, because it was an enormous building, a French Renaissance palace modelled on the Tuileries burnt down in the riots of 1871, and it stood within five minutes' walk of the main street. We went in, wondering how such a place came to be there. I bought a handbook and the first sentence of the curator's introduction seemed like mind-reading. 'Most people who pass through Barnard Castle will wonder at seeing such a magnificent building as the Bowes Museum in so small a town.' He then obviously felt compelled to justify his claim that the story of the museum's origin was an interesting one. This he did in the following discreetly-phrased sentences:

It was founded by John Bowes and his wife, Josephine Benoite Bowes, Countess of Montalbo. Mr Bowes was a son of the 10th Earl of Strathmore and Mary Milner, whose marriage did not take place until the day before the Earl's death in 1820. Their son, who was then eleven years of age, inherited the English estates of the family and in consequence, possessed considerable wealth.

The unorthodox philanthropist's museum passed the afternoon. Back in Mess, the evening high spirits of the subalterns were in startling contrast to their earlier lethargy. Their tastes ran to games with chairs which finished up in roars of laughter and two cases for the MO.

My bed was such that I did not in the least mind getting up before six o'clock next morning, though I might have been less eager had I known that I was going to be awake and in transit and still under military orders for the next thirty hours, non-stop.

At 8 a.m. we climbed into a three-ton truck and were driven to the main camp. As we scrambled down from the dirty lorry I noticed a group of German POWs gaping. There we were, eight officers, three of technically 'senior' rank, scrambling about in a truck, fending for ourselves and our baggage. The Wehrmacht, I felt, would have ordered things better. Not that I objected in the least to lorry-travel, but those staring blue eyes made me think suddenly of how surprising the scene must appear to them.

The second-in-command, a major of about my own age, inspected the parade of sixty NCOs and riflemen who were in our draft.

As we piled into the trucks again to go to the railway station I caught sight of a man who had been with me in 1940. He was a sergeant now. He told me where he had been and that he was now awaiting release. 'I came home from Africa compassionate,' he said. I asked why. With no change of expression in face or voice he said: 'I lost everything with a V2, sir; the wife, kids, home, everything.'

I said I was sorry, feeling as I said it that the words and tone were little different from those I would have used if he had told me he had had a bad headache. Embarrassed by my own inadequacy, I was glad to be called away because the truck was ready to start.

We had a two-hour wait at Darlington and when the York train came in the accommodation reserved for troops was already full.

At York we climbed into trucks again and drove out to Strensall Camp where, about three o'clock, a sergeant-major informed me solemnly that my dispersal centre would be London, something I had known for some time before I left London and which I might even have deduced for myself.

We had eight hours to pass at Strensall before being driven back to York to catch an after-midnight train for London. The transit Mess was like a dentist's waiting room or a residents' lounge in a modern roadhouse hotel. We sat round the fire in a wide semi-circle, talking desultorily, reading papers, doing crossword puzzles.

The bar opened at 6.15, so in preparation for this major social event I went through a door marked toilet. Matthews, who had sunk into a disgusted torpor of boredom, said he did not propose to bother washing. When I came back I remarked quietly to him that his decision might have been unhygienic but it was very sensible, as there was no soap, the water was freezing and the towel black. From a chair just behind, a clear, high-pitched voice said: 'Had you read the notice-board you would have known that the proper place to wash is at the other end, where there *are* soap and towels.' We sat up with a jerk. The speaker was a small, round-eyed man in battledress. He had an immature but thriving moustache and looked as if he was pushing manfully along the road towards looking like the popular conception of the British regular soldier. He was a major on the permanent staff of the camp.

I apologised for my ignorance, fighting down the instinct to be fairly rude, because I realised that basically I had committed the sin of criticising a Mess in which I was a visitor. It had not occurred to me that the Mess had members, that it was anything more than a military waiting room. Little Round-eyes looked rather scared after his outburst.

We paid a nominal twopence for a very good tea and eightpence for an excellent dinner in the Mess I had insulted. We drew a sandwich ration and as we sat shivering in our trucks at midnight on the misty parade ground a dim figure came round and pressed something into our hands. It was a threepenny piece. This, I found on enquiry, was the scale of allowance for refreshment during the night journey.

Our draft-conducting officer, now looking a little worn, cross-examined a sergeant-major closely about our reservations on the night train to London. The sergeant-major, a fine specimen whose features looked as though they had been carved out of sandstone by Giles, the cartoonist, was pained at the officer's scepticism. 'Sir,' he said, 'it's all laid on. It always is. We do it every day. The Railway Transport Officer will be on the platform and he knows you're coming. Absolutely all right, sir.'

The officer, remembering Darlington, was not convinced, which I thought a little unfair of him, but he was right. When the train came into York station at 1.10 a.m. there were no reserved compartments. Nor had the RTO been scented anywhere.

By good luck the train was not as full as we had feared and we all got seats. It was too cold to sleep. At 5.50 a.m. we reached King's Cross, and took another truck ride, this time to Regent's Park Barracks. Now (or at least after breakfast and that shave without which the British Army will very rightly not greet any dawn) the actual process of demobilisation began at last. It was quick, even slick. In half an hour we were demobilised—that is we were authorised to proceed on fifty-six days' leave, after which we would be relegated to the Unemployed (and unpaid) List until general demobilisation. We were interviewed by representatives of the War Office, the Pay Office (who gave me six shillings, for what I never troubled to find out), the Ministry of Labour and the Ministry of Health; we drew concession-rate cigarettes from NAAFI for our fifty-six days' leave, and then we were in a 'bus for Olympia and the civilian clothing issue.

The earlier release groups had oversold Olympia to us, I thought. There was a long dreary queue and the clothing, while body-covering, was aesthetically diabolical. I am not being superior about this. The men who went through the shirt and tie department with me were vociferous and unanimous in their criticism. The lighting was deceptive and the tie I had chosen because it was plain and seemed fairly dark in contrast with the maniacal designs around it, turned out to be an angry purple. The hats, I suspect, were plastic, and certainly fit only for a wet winter day in the depths of

206

the country, or throwing into the air expendably on cele-
bratory occasions.

However it was all better than being given a few pounds
and then waiting six months (which was par at that time) for
one's tailor to make a suit costing a great deal of money;
and anyhow it would have been difficult to depress or
seriously annoy me on such a day.

At home I put away my uniforms, Sam Browne belt and
cap, praying that I would never be called upon to don them
again. To go out to lunch I put on the suit which, I suddenly recalled, I had worn on that far-off day when I walked
out of my flat and joined the Army. And how far-off
September 3, 1939 seemed. Yet how vivid in memory. I
remembered Johnny Mills saying of the war, 'Do you think
it'll run?' when our uniforms were doled out to us, and I
realised that I had been longer in the Army than in any job
in my life till then. It seemed a century ago too since
Johnny had sat on the steps of a hut, polishing his buttons
and, without self-pity, saying that if the war went on long he
would never make the grade back to where he had stood as
an actor when it began. He had been mercifully wrong, for
now he was back in films and a bigger star than ever.

My other fellow-recruit, Anthony Pelissier, was back in
civilian life too, writing and directing in films and the
theatre, but in the interval he had performed the extraordinary feat of being invalided out of the Army, qualifying
for his master's certificate, and commanding a ship in the
Merchant Navy before being invalided out again.

I was going back to my pre-war job in Fleet Street and
when the three of us met again it would be difficult to believe
that the things that had happened to us in the interval were
really true.

Then I was out in the familiar streets of Chelsea for the
first time as a post-war civilian, flexing my shoulders
luxuriously in my old suit and breathing deep, intoxicating

breaths of peacetime air. The wheels of the 'bus that took me to the West End gave out a beautiful, tuneful rhythm to which the only refrain was 'I'm out of the Army now, I'm out of the Army now.'

Technically, I suppose, I wasn't quite; not for fifty-six days yet. But after six years and six weeks it was near enough not to quibble.

[Continued from front flap]

"Some men are overwhelmed by the evils and horrors of war, and their experience is an essential part of its total reality; there are others to whom war reveals, to their own surprise, unexpected gifts of service and, in the sense of trying to do well things they are by nature unfitted to do, of self-sacrifice. Mr. Watts is one of these . . . and therefore his reminiscences of war have a kind of truth which many more pretentious books often miss."

In *Moonlight on a Lake in Bond Street* Mr. Watts, a drama critic and contributor to the *New Yorker*, blends humor and drama with a warm understanding of those millions whose nature is civilian and whose lot for so long was military.

CPSIA information can be obtained
at www.ICGtesting.com
Printed in the USA
BVHW052350080223

658190BV00005B/123